Preaching the Beatitudes for the Glory of God

Preaching the Beatitudes for the Glory of God

LANDIS BROWN

Foreword by Andrew Curry

WIPF & STOCK · Eugene, Oregon

PREACHING THE BEATITUDES FOR THE GLORY OF GOD

Copyright © 2025 Landis Brown. All rights reserved. Except for brief quotations in critical publications or reviews, no part of this book may be reproduced in any manner without prior written permission from the publisher. Write: Permissions, Wipf and Stock Publishers, 199 W. 8th Ave., Suite 3, Eugene, OR 97401.

Wipf & Stock
An Imprint of Wipf and Stock Publishers
199 W. 8th Ave., Suite 3
Eugene, OR 97401

www.wipfandstock.com

PAPERBACK ISBN: 979-8-3852-3078-5
HARDCOVER ISBN: 979-8-3852-3079-2
EBOOK ISBN: 979-8-3852-3080-8

VERSION NUMBER 01/15/25

Unless otherwise indicated, Scripture quotations are from the King James Version.

Scripture quotations marked ESV are from The Holy Bible, English Standard Version (ESV), Text Edition 2016, copyright © 2001 by Crossway Bible, a publishing ministry of Good News Publishers. All Rights Reserved

Excerpts from *The Sermon on the Mount and Human Flourishing* by Jonathan T. Pennington, copyright © 2017. Used by permission of Baker Academic, a division of Baker Publishing Group.

Contents

Foreword by Andrew Curry | vii
Preface | ix

Section One: A Correct View of *Makarios* Leads to a Correct View of the Beatitudes

1. Introduction | 3
2. Cultural Context of the Sermon on the Mount | 6
3. Literary Features and Context | 15
4. Alternate Views of the Beatitudes | 23
5. Interpreting the Word "Blessed" and *Makarios* | 28
6. *Bārûk* vs. *'Asrê* | 42
7. *Teleios* and *Makarios* | 49
8. Conclusion | 54

Section Two: Four Dominant Views in Preaching the Beatitudes

9. Introduction | 61
10. God's Favor/Entrance Requirements | 64
11. Eschatological Reversal Blessings | 69
12. Wisdom or Virtue Ethics Reading | 72
13. Blending Views of Beatitudes for Proper Preaching | 76
14. Conclusion | 84

Section Three: Preaching the Beatitudes for the Glory of God

15 Introduction | 89
16 *Macarisms* and Other Scriptures | 90
17 Do the Beatitudes Contradict Society's View of Flourishing? | 93
18 Biblical Standards for Flourishing | 96
19 Beatitudes Positive or Negative | 99
20 Beatitudes Considering the Old Testament | 104
21 Conclusion | 109

Bibliography | 111

Foreword

COULD THERE BE A better sermon for a preacher to think on than the Sermon on the Mount? Yet, this masterpiece delivered by the One who taught with authority is arguably the most misapplied section of Scripture by modern pastors. Landis is himself a preacher and wrote this book out of the desire that this text would be preached as an invitation to human flourishing rather than a hammer to beat congregants over the head with. Leaning on the belief that God's word is effective, he encourages us to read Scripture carefully to ensure God's true message is delivered and applied as a balm to the soul of the Christian in the pew.

Landis dissuades an aggressive handling of the text that would hurt the congregation, or a handling that would foster a pharisaical mindset, content to behave as "Christians" though one's heart is hard. Instead, by focusing on the intention of the text, Landis proposes the Beatitudes help one understand their position before God, draws the heart towards greater Christ dependence, and encourages true Christian flourishing even as we live in a fallen world.

The first major section of the work shows that God's instruction is not just one of dry theory but one that cultivates understanding of one's heart and encourages one to live in a way that would allow true human flourishing and joy as the individual seeks to live according to God's design.

Foreword

The practical discussion in section two demonstrates that one's interpretation affects one's preaching practice. This section provides a means of self-examination so that the preacher may consider the message they herald and the extent to which it reflects the biblical text. This reading, alongside section three, encourages intentionality in the heart of the preacher that will promote both purpose and direction when proclaiming this treasured section of Scripture from the pulpit.

I am grateful for the research and reflection presented in this work. I believe it will be of benefit to earnest pastors seeking to communicate God's encouragement to the saints. This is a preaching text drawn from the heart of a preacher who wants simply to feed Christ's lambs.

> Study to shew thyself approved unto God, a workman that needeth not to be ashamed, rightly dividing the word of truth. (2 Tim 2:15)

Andrew Curry

Preface

THE SERMON ON THE Mount is one of the most excellent sermons preached by the greatest preacher ever to live, our Lord Jesus Christ. Interwoven within the Sermon on the Mount are many literary genres that allow the preacher to formulate his sermons in many ways. Within the Sermon on the Mount are literary genres such as wisdom literature, narration, exhortations, indicative statements, parables, and many others that will not allow the preacher to become bored when preaching through this beautiful sermon. Essentially, when preaching through the Sermon on the Mount, the preacher is preaching another preacher's sermon, and it just so happens to be Christ's sermon.

First, this book aims to give the proper hermeneutic of the Beatitudes which are presented at the beginning of the Sermon on the Mount. While writing this book, I assumed that the reader already knows the mechanics of expository preaching. I assume the reader knows how to exegete, outline, and deliver the text. At the beginning of this book, I argue that once a preacher grasps how to interpret the Beatitudes, he will effectively preach them, pointing people to Christ and his finished work on the cross; the results of his work are the manifestation of the Beatitudes in the believer's life.

I have enjoyed the many ways the Beatitudes have been preached by folks with different preaching styles from mine, however I have not enjoyed some of the ways they have been preached

Preface

by folks who did not have a proper hermeneutic when interpreting the Beatitudes. Many times, I have sat under what we in the South call "hard preaching," where the Beatitudes were presented as a list of commandments rather than indicative statements. This book argues against the legalistic preaching of the Beatitudes that present each as commandments to receive God's favor. This book will instead reveal that the statements presented within the Beatitudes are indicative statements of fact painting a picture of authentic believers and the promises they have due their salvation and citizenship in the kingdom of heaven. The Beatitudes will be revealed as promise statements that cannot be revoked and that offer the congregation to whom you will be preaching a present hope due to currently being a part of the kingdom of heaven (Matt 5:3) and a future hope of eventually seeing God (Matt 5:8).

The breakdown of this book is simple with only three main sections with chapters included in each section. The sections are as follows: Section one examines the Greek word *makarios* and its relation to the Old Testament Hebrew words *'asrê* and *baruk*. Section one's argument for *makarios* being better understood as a state of flourishing rather than a bestowed blessing relies heavily on Jonathan Pennington's study of the Greek word *makarios* and its use in the Septuagint in his book *The Sermon on the Mount and Human Flourishing*. This section strives to properly understand the Greek word *makarios* using semantics and pragmatics to see if the word "blessed" is a proper English gloss. A proper understanding of the word *makarios* within the Beatitudes will encourage believers by giving them a profile of who they are in Christ along with all the promises that come along with being in Christ. Interpreting the Beatitudes correctly shows believers there is ample reason to live a flourishing life now even in a fallen world due to their position in Christ and the promises that come along with that position. It is my hope that this section will help believers finally have assurance and rest in their salvation, allowing them to live a flourishing life due to the promises guaranteed to each believer in each beatific statement.

Section two will examine three dominant interpretations of the Beatitudes as mentioned by Jonathan Pennington in his book

Preface

The Sermon on the Mount and Human Flourishing. This section will give examples of how each view or interpretation is reflected in one's sermon. Section two will wrap up providing a fourth interpretation of the Beatitudes, which is a blend of the three views that Pennington mentions. This fourth interpretation mentioned provides a proper hermeneutic for preachers to preach the Beatitudes in such a way that offers hope and encouragement to believers while glorifying God's sovereignty over salvation.

Section three will attempt to explain how other parts of Scripture confirm the statements presented in the Beatitudes as promises Christ gives to those who are already his followers. The aim of section three is to offer a guide to preaching the Beatitudes as positive affirmations to those living in a falling world. I hope this small book will help preachers grasp the text of the Beatitudes more accurately, thus providing an accurate presentation of the Beatitudes to their congregations. I also hope the preaching of the Beatitudes that you will eventually perform will encourage your congregants by showing them they can flourish now in a fallen world because of who they are in Christ and have continual joy for God's future kingdom.

Section One

A Correct View of *Makarios* Leads to a Correct View of the Beatitudes

1

Introduction

It was the rich young ruler who came to Christ in Mark 10:17–27, asking Jesus, "What shall I do to inherit eternal life?" This account provides the reader a glimpse of a man who thought that his merit would earn him God's blessings. This is the same mindset of those who view the Beatitudes as rules that, if followed, will cause them to inherit God's present and future blessings. Wealthy and owning much property, the rich young ruler would not like the answer that Christ gives to his question. Christ answers with devastating directions rather than affirmation, telling the young man to rid himself of all his wealth and give it to the poor while taking up his cross and following Christ to inherit eternal life. By secular standards, this man should have had a flourishing and prosperous life, however he felt that he lacked one thing: eternal life, which could only be derived from a conventual relationship with Christ. He tells Christ that he followed all God's commandments as laid out in the Mosaic law, hoping that God would bless him with eternal life based on this merit. This man did not understand that earthly riches could not give him true happiness and peace; he also did not understand that God does not bless based on merit or morality.

Section One: A Correct View of *Makarios* Leads to a Correct View

The mindset of the rich young ruler is seen today in those who regard true happiness and entering the kingdom of God as something obtained by merit. Like the rich young ruler, some believe that by their merit, they deserve blessings and favor from God, assuming that the accumulation of earthly riches will offer them true happiness. Jonathan Pennington, professor of New Testament at The Southern Baptist Theological Seminary, points out in his book *The Sermon on the Mount and Human Flourishing* that the reason why the rich young ruler was not able to inherit eternal life is that he "lacked *teleios* righteousness."[1] According to Pennington, *teleios* is more than just being perfect in the sense of not breaking God's law; it is having a wholistic relationship with God, an intimate "covenant relationship" that stems from following God.[2] Christ desires this young man to follow him wholeheartedly, requiring him to get rid of the materialistic things he believes bring him true happiness. He is to replace these riches with Christ, which will lead to a true flourishing life.

The Beatitudes have been mistakenly interpreted much like the rich young ruler's interpretation of how to inherit eternal life. The reading of the Beatitudes often makes one assume that the promises within each are a part of a rewards-based system that is rooted in merit. To some, if a person follows the Beatitudes as a list of things to achieve, then that person will have blessings bestowed upon them by God. In his book *The Kingdom of God and the Church*, Geerhardus Johannes Vos, a Dutch-American Calvinist theologian and former representative of the Princeton theology, refutes this reward system when he writes, "The first thing to remember is that we have no right to declare the desire for reward as a motive in ethical conduct unworthy of a high standard of morality and therefore unworthy of the better element in our Lord's teaching."[3] Thus the interpretation of the Beatitudes should not have its foundation in desiring to act on what the Beatitudes present only to receive a reward. This reward system based on merit

---

1. Pennington, *Sermon on the Mount*, 273.
2. Pennington, *Sermon on the Mount*, 73.
3. Vos, *Kingdom of God*, 102.

Introduction

often stems from the mistranslation of the word *Makarios* at the beginning of each Beatitude.

The word "blessed" is a mistranslation of the word *Makarios*, leading to a misinterpretation of the Beatitudes. The word "blessed," as seen at the beginning of each of the nine Beatitudes, can be confusingly taken to mean "a bestowed favor" upon those who act according to what the Beatitudes portray. This interpretation breeds a legalistic approach to inheriting eternal life. This section will refute the interpretation that the Beatitudes are a list of qualities to strive for to receive God's blessing or favor. This improper interpretation is born from the weak English gloss "blessed," which is used in most English translations for the word *makarios*. This section will seek to examine the Greek word *makarios*, proving that the English gloss blessed is weak which leads to confusion and should be replaced with a word describing a state of being. By examining the English gloss "blessed" along with the Greek word *makarios*, this section will attempt to conclude that the Greek word *makarios* is properly rendered as describing a state of being, specifically flourishing or happiness, rather than a bestowed blessing from God. To examine the Beatitudes more closely, cultural context must be considered first.

2

Cultural Context of the Sermon on the Mount

THERE ARE TWO CONTEXTS to consider that are blended in the world of Matthew's Gospel. First, Matthew's Gospel is rooted in a Second Temple Jewish context. Secondly, the Sermon on the Mount also lies within the Greco-Roman context. Both aspects of these contexts are blended in the Gospel of Matthew. Each context also brings its flavor in the interpretation of the Sermon on the Mount, particularly the Beatitudes. Christ's teaching within the Sermon was most likely interpreted by those from both contexts, with a mixture of a crowd who took Christ's sermon as both wisdom and ethical directions. The Sermon on the Mount draws from and activates the dominant parts of both contexts, which will help us understand why the Beatitudes were viewed in a legalistic manner even during the time they were given.[1] Paul Johannes du Plessis says in his book *Teleios: The Idea of Perfection in the New Testament* that "not considering the dual context of the New Testament would be a futile attempt at theology as playing on a one-string violin is

---

1. Pennington, *Human Flourishing*, 35.

a poor array of music."[2] Plessis is correct that proper exegesis of any passage, including the Sermon on the Mount, must be done in light of its historical context.

Second Temple Jewish Context

At the heart of Second Temple Jewish culture was the hope of God's restoration of the lost kingdom of God that had been dissolved after the fall of humanity in the garden of Eden. Humanity was allowed to flourish and live a life of true prosperity within the garden of Eden not long after the first acts of creation. In Gen 2, God plants man in the garden of Eden to nourish it and have dominion over all his creation but not without a warning to not eat of the tree of knowledge of good and evil. This commandment would quickly be disregarded and broken by the end of Gen 2. By the end of chapter 3 of Genesis, Adam and Eve's disobedience to God's commandments, humankind's first acts of sin, threw God's creation into oblivion and wrecked creation's state of flourishing. Genesis 3 depicts humankind's failing to love God wholeheartedly, ushering in the punishment of death, depravity, and the need for salvation. From the fall of man to the Sermon on the Mount, God's restoration of his kingdom back to the state in which it was founded in Eden has been desired amongst the Jewish culture.[3] Pennington claims that the fall of man and the desire for God's restored kingdom "are the backdrop and props of the stage on which the dramatic story of Jesus, Christianity, and the New Testament writings are played out."[4] This hope of a restored kingdom is often seen in the effort placed by many within the Old Testament to follow God's commandments. The Jewish context of the Old Testament proves that merit played a significant role in hoping that God would bless them with this new kingdom that would allow them to live a flourishing life. The hope of a life that would be rid of disease,

---

2. Plessis, *Teleios*, 35.
3. Plessis, *Teleios*, 35
4. Pennington, *Human Flourishing*, 25.

Section One: A Correct View of *Makarios* Leads to a Correct View

suffering, labor, and death had been lost in the garden event in Gen 3. Second Temple Jews desired a restored kingdom of God as much as those before them, but how they would receive this restored kingdom was based on their merit and how they could usher it in by living a particular lifestyle.

The setting of the Sermon on the Mount is called the era of Second Temple Judaism which lies between the return from exile in Babylon to the rededication of the Second Temple to the eventual destruction of the temple for a second time around AD 70. Those Jews writing during this time and seeking a restored kingdom of God considered themselves living in the "Second Temple age."[5] This time offers a foundation for why the Second Temple Jews interpreted the Beatitudes differently.

The Second Temple age marked the growing genre of wisdom literature within the Jewish community. This wisdom literature would act as a springboard for interpreting apocalyptic writings and as a guide for being a part of this future restored kingdom. According to Pennington, "This wisdom-apocalyptic thread of Jewish literature provides a particularly important encyclopedic context for understanding the sermon, especially the Beatitudes."[6] Second Temple Jews interpret wisdom literature as a guide to living a life that would result in true happiness and prosperity. Second Temple Jews viewed Proverbs as a manual for life, believing that if they lived according to the wisdom presented in Proverbs, God would bestow upon them blessings that would result in a prosperous life. Although the Second Temple Jews had good intentions in desiring a flourishing life, unfortunately, it would only be obtained through their efforts and God's recognition of those efforts. Their reward of a prosperous, flourishing lifestyle was based on how morally intact they were and how closely they aligned themselves with the wisdom literature presented in books such as Proverbs and others containing wisdom literature. Pennington observes that the wisdom literature, which guided the Second Temple Jews, was filled with "nitty-gritty details of how to live life in a way that will result

---

5. Pennington, *Human Flourishing*, 58.
6. Pennington, *Human Flourishing*, 26.

in peace and happiness with the instructions as diverse as how to handle money, to the approach of young men should take regarding young women, to how to deal with foolish people."[7] Second Temple Jewish wisdom literature includes reflections on existence, justice, life's meaning, and the overall human experience that leads to a life blessed by God.[8] This type of literature is foundational in how the Second Temple Jews determined how to obtain a flourishing life.

Pennington argues that Second Temple Jews viewed virtue as means to achieve a life of happiness and blessings from God.[9] This virtue that was desired by Second Temple Jews was rooted in the nature of God and not in the ideal human virtue. God was the example and standard of virtue in whom the Second Temple Jews wished to emulate. To have a flourishing life begins, according to wisdom literature, particularly in Prov 1, with a "fear of Yahweh." God is the basis and the example which one must follow to achieve morality and thus gain blessings as rewards. According to Jacob Neusner, scholar of Judaic literature, "At the center of wisdom literature is the idea that religious devotion, the fear of the Lord, preceded all knowledge and is indeed final as well."[10] It is thus the virtue or the quality of a person's life that leads to blessings from God. As the restored kingdom of God approaches, a person's virtue must be perfect; it must be up to par with the standards God has set in his wisdom literature. These standards and directions are to be lived out with the hope of the reward of eternal bliss with God. Also, these standards are to be met based on the outward acts of those commands presented within the wisdom literature. The heart of man with this mindset is left burdened by relying on his actions to achieve God's blessings rather than salvation that God has already achieved for them through the person and work of his Son Jesus Christ.

Wisdom literature and apocalyptic literature were heavily related in Second Temple Jewish culture. Apocalyptic literature

7. Pennington, *Human Flourishing*, 26.
8. Neusner and Green, *Dictionary of Judaism*, 672.
9. Pennington, *Human Flourishing*, 26.
10. Neusner and Green, *Dictionary of Judaism*, 672.

Section One: A Correct View of *Makarios* Leads to a Correct View

was fused with wisdom literature due to the hope of entering a coming restored kingdom based on following the directions given in wisdom literature. This hope for a restored kingdom of God stems from such places within Scripture as Ezek 36:35, where Ezekiel prophesies saying, "And they shall say, This land that was desolate is become like the garden of Eden; and the waste and desolate and ruined cities are become fenced, and are inhabited." Other examples of this hope of a restored state of the kingdom of God are seen in Isa 51:3, where Isaiah prophesies saying, "For the LORD shall comfort Zion; he will comfort all her waste places; and he will make her wilderness like Eden, and her desert like the garden of the LORD; joy and gladness shall be found therein, thanksgiving, and the voice of melody." These verses show that the Second Temple Jews looked forward to a restored kingdom which had been stripped from them. They trusted that if they followed the commandments presented in the Torah and the wisdom literature, they would receive the benefits of this restored kingdom of God. Dale Allison Jr., professor of New Testament at Princeton Seminary, speaks correctly regarding the reinforcement of morality within the Jewish community. Allison states,

> The expectation of a new world entails the end of the present world and of its conventional customs and social arrangements, and if those customs and arrangements are soon to go, one's present way of life can hardly continue as ever. One rather is strongly encouraged to become, in anticipation, less tied to the present state of the world.[11]

Morality that has resulted in separation from the current world is not due to man's efforts or will but is due to God's grace in his sanctification process. Second Temple Jews desired to be separated from the world by looking to wisdom literature as directions to follow to achieve separation. In doing so, however, the separation and blessings rely solely on their efforts rather than God. This view of following God's commandments to receive rewarded blessings eventually leads to legalism. It seems that interpreting the

11. Allison et al., *Recover What Has Been Lost*, 297.

Beatitudes as wisdom literature is correct; however, the intentions behind achieving what the Beatitudes present are where most get it wrong. Like the Second Temple Jews, some viewed the Beatitudes as specific directions to follow regarding a lifestyle change that, if done correctly, will result in a person receiving blessings from God, including being a part of his future kingdom. Again, this interpretation relies heavily on a reward-based system, where the closer a person gets to emulating a Beatitude, the more they will be blessed.

Greco-Roman Context

Another context in which the Sermon on the Mount is presented is the Greco-Roman culture of Christ's day. The Greco-Roman context in which Matthew's Gospel was heavily influenced by moral philosophy and human effort. This moral philosophy sculpted how some of Christ's listeners would have viewed his statements presented within the Beatitudes. Many would consider his statements moral or ethical goals that would lead to a life of true happiness. Greco-Roman philosophy sought to answer the question of how to achieve true happiness. Those of the Greco-Roman culture desired to achieve happiness that would not be temporary or based on a current circumstance but happiness that would be eternal, no matter the circumstance.

With this view in mind, those around Christ looked at wisdom literature such as the Beatitudes as moral directions to obtain an eternal state of happiness through human effort. The Greeks sought the answer to true happiness, which in their minds stemmed from having perfect morality. Hans Deiter Betz, a former professor at the University of Chicago, provides a great analysis of the Sermon on the Mount that shows how it was influenced and interpreted within a Greco-Roman context. In Betz's analysis of the Sermon on the Mount, he concludes that the form and function of the Sermon are closely related to "Hellenistic moral philosophical works."[12] Those of Hellenistic tradition would interpret Christ's Sermon, specifically

---

12. Betz, *Sermon on the Mount*, 16.

Section One: A Correct View of *Makarios* Leads to a Correct View

the Beatitudes, as moral literature that provides the framework for achieving true happiness through morality.

As the Greeks sought to find an answer to what makes people truly happy, many answers came from Greek philosophers such as Socrates. Socrates was amongst the first to assert that happiness is derived from human effort. Philosophers such as Socrates concluded that some type of moral perfection through human effort would offer someone a more extraordinary life of true happiness. It seems that many contemporary commentators follow in the same lines as the Greco-Roman thought regarding the Beatitudes as a list of entrance requirements that one must perform to be able to enter into the kingdom of God.[13] With this Greco-Roman context of seeking true happiness through human effort, Robert Guelich has heard many comments about how the Sermon on the Mount, specifically the Beatitudes, is a list of practical ways to live. Guelich says, "On the practical level, one frequently hears comments to the effect of trying to 'live according to the Sermon on the Mount.' This generally means orienting one's attitudes and conduct by the various Beatitudes; the Beatitudes have become an ideal for human conduct, a goal to be pursued."[14] This approach to the Beatitudes that is heavily influenced by Greco-Roman moral tradition sparks "a sense of guilt or inadequacy,"[15] which in turn leads to legalism in search of happiness. Thus, those who interpret the Beatitudes through a Greco-Roman context only are considered in error due to emphasis on humankind's efforts alone in obtaining true happiness rather than Christ being the source of eternal bliss. This state of happiness that is derived from human effort, including moral philosophies such as virtue ethics, is called in the Greek *eudaimonia*, which, according to Pennington, is best translated as "human flourishing."[16] *Eudaimonia* is thus thought to be achievable through human effort and the attempt to meet the requirements listed in wisdom literature.

13. Guelich, *Foundation for Understanding*, 109–11.
14. Guelich, *Foundation for Understanding*, 109–11.
15. Guelich, *Foundation for Understanding*, 109–11.
16. Pennington, *Human Flourishing*, 32.

Cultural Context of the Sermon on the Mount

Blended Context

Within the Gospel of Matthew, both Greco-Roman and Second Temple Jewish culture are blended. Wisdom literature is seen as a set of directions or standards by which a person achieves the proper state of morality, thus receiving God's blessing of true happiness. Therefore, this blessing is only bestowed upon the person who achieves the morality standard presented within the wisdom literature provided. The blending of the contexts provides an idea that if someone properly sustains the morality that is given within the Sermon on the Mount, then that person will receive happiness through blessings from God. Robert Guelich recognizes this error in the blending of the contexts when he says,

> For Matthew, these Beatitudes were not intended to be benedictions that pronounce one blessed in a sacral rite, nor did they intend to express popular wisdom or ethical teaching of that day. Rather, these are to be heard and understood as having been spoken by the one who came to fulfill the Law and the Prophets. Instead of ethics swallowing up eschatology in Matthew, we have just the reverse. The implicit attitudes and conduct of the Beatitudes, as well as the demands of Matthew 5:20–48, are only intelligible, considering that Jesus's person and ministry established a new eschatological moment between God and humanity.[17]

The blending of wisdom literature to achieve a standard of morality which would bring about countless blessings bled over into the religious sects of Christ's day. The Pharisees, who were heavily religious, viewed the teachings of the Torah as wisdom literature that provided a standard of morality that would bring about bestowed blessings from God. With the blend of contexts, the Pharisees would err in seeking true happiness by emphasizing the external actions of morality rather than focusing on their hearts.[18] Since the Pharisees had this blended view that misguided them in

---

17. Guelich, *Foundation for Understanding*, 109.
18. Pennington, *Human Flourishing*, 7.

Section One: A Correct View of *Makarios* Leads to a Correct View

interpreting God's law, Christ would say to them in Matt 23:27, "Woe unto you, scribes and Pharisees, hypocrites! For ye are like unto whited sepulchers, which indeed appear beautiful outward, but are within full of dead men's bones, and of all uncleanness." The Pharisees' approach to wisdom literature such as the Sermon on the Mount is that of seeking a standard of morality that would lead to God's bestowed blessings upon them. This view has been carried over in many generations after the Second Temple Jewish period and is seen today in the commentaries of those who view the Beatitudes as moral standards that, if achieved, will allow them to receive God's blessing; however, this is not what Jesus intended when giving the Beatitudes. Rather than the Beatitudes presenting ethical standards that are to be achieved, they instead indicate ethical standards that result from one who has been changed by Christ through salvation, offering a sort of profile for genuine believers, namely those who are flourishing because of the promise indicated at the end of each Beatitude. Jesus in his teachings within the Beatitudes went against the grain to show that it was not by human effort or morality that the kingdom of heaven is obtained but rather through a conventual relationship with God. Other alternative views of the Beatitudes still exist today with a backdrop of both Second Temple Jewish and Greco-Roman thought spawning a moral ethical flavor as their interpretative foundation, thus viewing the Beatitudes as standards to meet rather than standards that are acquired upon salvation. Although the remainder of the Sermon on the Mount can be viewed as wisdom literature, namely on how to live in a fallen world as kingdom citizens, the literary features of the Beatitudes show they are separate in their purpose from the rest of the discourse. The Beatitudes are separate from them in their function from the remainder of the Sermon in that they profile believers as being in a state of flourishing because of their status as kingdom citizens rather than directions on how to achieve blessings.

3

Literary Features and Context

Boundary Markers

DISTINGUISHABLE BY BOUNDARY MARKERS, the Sermon on the Mount is a separate discourse from the rest of the events that Matthew or Luke describe in the life of Christ. Even further, the Beatitudes stand alone in their purpose within the Sermon on the Mount. While the Sermon on the Mount apart from the Beatitudes has its fair share of imperatives, the Beatitudes are constructed with indicative statements that explain the characteristics of believers. While the Sermon on the Mount acts as wisdom literature guiding its listeners on how to live as God's kingdom citizens, the Beatitudes instead provides a profile of those citizens, namely that they are those who are *makarioi*. Therefore, the literary features of both the Sermon on the Mount and the Beatitudes further validate that the Beatitudes are not a list of commands as the rest of the Sermon on the Mount but stand alone as indicative statements profiling the life and characteristics of genuine believers.

The Sermon on the Mount begins in chapter 5 of Matthew's Gospel and chapter 6 in the Gospel according to Luke. Matthew, however, provides a starting point for Jesus's sermon in Matt 5:2

Section One: A Correct View of *Makarios* Leads to a Correct View

using the participle *anoixas*. *Anoixas* is a nominative masculine singular aorist active participle derived from the lemma *anoigo*, meaning "to cause something to be open—'to open, to make open.'"[1] *Anoixas* is a circumstantial participle "that is so much a part of the main clause that it is best translated as a main verb."[2] In his Greek grammar, *It's Still Greek to Me*, David Allan Black claims that such participles of "attendant circumstance [are] used both to introduce a new action and to focus attention on the main verb."[3] In this case, the participle *anoixas* acts as the main verb of the sentence, indicating a new course of action that Jesus is performing with his disciples, marking a new section in Jesus's ministry. *Anoixas* is confirmed as a circumstantial participle by Black's classification of these types of participles: "In this construction, the tense of the participle is usually aorist as is the tense of the main verb."[4] Thus, since *anoixas* is in the aorist tense, acting as the main verb and describing a new course of action that Jesus is performing, then *anoixas* acts as a true circumstantial participle. Therefore, Matt 5:2 marks the beginning of Jesus's discourse of the Sermon on the Mount.

This new course of action Jesus takes with his disciples is further confirmed by the action that immediately follows the circumstantial participle. Jesus not only sits down with his disciples in Matt 5:1, but he opens his mouth (*anoixas*) and begins to teach (*edidasken*) them. *Edidasken* is an imperfect, active, indicative, third-person, singular verb that is an ingressive imperfect. As in the ingressive imperfect verb, *edidasken* also marks the beginning of a new action. Daniel Wallace states in his Greek grammar, *Greek Grammar Beyond the Basics*, "The imperfect is often used to stress the beginning of an action, with the implication that it continued for some time."[5] Wallace continues, confirming that the ingressive imperfect marks a new beginning of a course of actions, stating, "Semantically the ingressive imperfect is especially used in

---

1. Louw and Nida, *Greek-English Lexicon*, 703.
2. Grant Osbourne, *Matthew*, 165.
3. Black, *It's Still Greek to Me*, 164.
4. Black, *It's Still Greek to Me*, 164.
5. Wallace, *Greek Grammar*, 544.

Literary Features and Context

narrative literature when a change in activity is noted, introducing a topic shift."[6] Thus, Matt 5:2 offers a beginning point for the discourse that Jesus is about to give regarding the entirety of the Sermon on the Mount and the Beatitudes, which lie at the beginning of the Sermon on the Mount.

The ending of the Beatific discourse at the beginning of the Sermon on the Mount is marked by the ending of the use of the predicate adjective *makarioi* which serves as its own boundary marker for the beginning of each Beatitude. The use of *hymeis* at the beginning of verse 13 marks the ending of the cohesion that was present within verses 3–13 (Beatitudes) through the repetitious use of the adjective *makarioi*. Also, the structure of verse 13 differs from that of the previous verses in that it does not have independent and subordinate clauses. Also, verse 13 is not considered a first-class conditional sentence like the previous sentences in verses 3–12. However, according to Wallace, verse 13 contains an independent clause, categorized as an asyndeton.[7] Verse 13 also includes a second independent clause, this time contrastive to the first, connected by a coordinating conjunction. The asyndeton independent clause in verse 13 reveals that verse 13 is unrelated to previous verses and acts as a "topic shift"[8] in the discourse.

In the Beatitudes, Jesus is not only profiling believers as *makarioi*, but in each subordinate clause, he offers an explanation as to why they are blessed or more appropriately able to flourish using the conjunction *hoti*. Verse 13 uses a single clause to describe believers as "salt of the earth," marking a new section in Christ's description of believers. Verse 13 seems to leave the repetition of first-class conditional statements in verses 3–12 and offers a third-class conditional statement. According to Wallace, a third-class conditional statement presents "the condition as uncertain of fulfillment."[9] In verse 13, the phrase "but if the salt have lost his savour, wherewith shall it be salted" is considered a third-class conational statement.

6. Wallace, *Greek Grammar*, 544.
7. Wallace, *Greek Grammar*, 658.
8. Wallace, *Greek Grammar*, 658.
9. Wallace, *Greek Grammar*, 696.

Section One: A Correct View of *Makarios* Leads to a Correct View

Verse 13 presents a hypothetical and unlikely situation in which salt loses its flavor, denoting that Christians, as the salt of the earth, should not lose their saltiness. Thus, the structure and topic of verse 13 marks a good ending of the discourse in verses 3–12. Therefore, the Beatitudes are considered a micro-discourse amongst the macro of the Sermon on the Mount, not only different literarily but in its function, namely to serve as a profile for believers rather than directions as the rest of the Sermon on the Mount assumes. Although the boundary marker for the Beatitudes ends at the beginning of verse 13, it and the rest of the Sermon on the Mount share some aspects of literary form.

Cohesion Within the Beatitudes

Independent and Dependent Clauses

Further indication that the Beatitudes are separate in form and function from the rest of the Sermon on the Mount is presented in the way they are tied together. In his book *Advances in the Study of Greek*, Constantine Campbell provides a simple definition of cohesion as far its relation to linguistics. Campbell asserts, "Cohesion refers to the way in which a text hangs together."[10] Thus, examining the cohesion of how the Beatitudes "hang together" will further show their separation in their purpose from the rest of the Sermon on the Mount. Cohesion is present within the Beatitudes due to using a series of similar independent clauses. Each beginning of the Beatitudes starts with an asyndeton independent clause followed by an adverbial clause. *Makarioi hoi ptochoi to pneumati* ("blessed are the poor in spirit") at the beginning of Matt 5:3 is considered an asyndeton because it marks the start of a series of other Beatific statements.[11] The independent clauses presented in each Beatitude differ from most independent clauses within the Sermon on the Mount because a conjunctive word or phrase does not introduce them. However, each Beatitude's dependent clause is considered

---

10. Campbell, *Study of Greek*, 152–53.
11. Wallace, *Greek Grammar*, 696.

Literary Features and Context

a conjunctive clause because they are introduced with a conjunction.[12] Each dependent clause in the Beatitudes is a definite relative clause because each contains a verb in the indicative mood and refers to a specific group of people, namely believers. According to Wallace, there are "three broad syntactical functions to dependent clauses: substantival, adjectival, and adverbial."[13] The dependent clauses in each Beatitude are adverbial clauses indicating a cause. The construction of each Beatitude's dependent clause begins with *hoti* plus the indicative, indicating the cause of why believers are *makarioi* as presented in the independent clause. Therefore, there is cohesion in the beatific section of the Sermon on the Mount due to the construction of each statement as having both an asyndeton independent clause and an adverbial dependent clause.

Subordinating Conjunctions

The Beatitudes are also in cohesion due to the conjunctions present within each. Conjunctions are essential because they relate the thoughts of a passage to one another.[14] The conjunction *hoti* is used nine times within the Beatitudes, connecting each independent clause with its subordinate clause. *Hoti* explains why believers are in a state of human flourishing or blessedness. Thus, Matt 5:3 could be translated as "Blessed are those who are poor in spirit because [*hoti*] theirs is the kingdom of Heaven." *Hoti* is considered a subordinate conjunction because the indicative mood governs it.[15] *Hoti* acts explicitly as an explanatory conjunction that "provides additional information about what is being described."[16] In the case of the Beatitudes, *hoti* can also be described as a causal conjunction because it expresses the basis of why believers are in a state of *makarios*. *Hoti* is subordinating in nature, "joining a

---

12. Wallace, *Greek Grammar*, 659.
13. Wallace, *Greek Grammar*, 660.
14. Wallace, *Greek Grammar*, 668.
15. Wallace, *Greek Grammar*, 668.
16. Wallace, *Greek Grammar*, 673.

subordinate element to the principal element of the sentence,"[17] namely why are believers *makarioi*. The use of *hoti* also repeatedly functions as an organic tie, namely that of hypotaxis, because it draws a "relation between an independent item and an item that is dependent on it."[18] There is a subordinate hypotaxis relationship between those who are blessed and the ones having the kingdom of heaven as theirs.

Conditional Statements

The Beatitudes are also connected through first-class conditional statements in each. Each statement describes a reality that believers are *makarios hoti* of the assumed true condition they are in or will be in at the end of each Beatitude. In Matt 5:3, for example, the protasis of the sentence is the clause giving the condition in a conditional statement, namely the condition of those who are *makarioi* because they are poor in spirit. In the case of "blessed are the poor in spirit, for theirs is the kingdom of heaven," the protasis is "blessed are the poor in spirit," while the apodosis, the consequent clause of a conditional sentence, would be "theirs is the kingdom of heaven." Each Beatitude, such as the one presented in Matt 5:3, portrays the reality that all believers share because they are poor in spirit. The reality is that believers are *makarioi hoti*: they currently have the kingdom of heaven as theirs.

Repetitious Words

Another connecting point in the Beatitudes is its repetitious use of the predicate adjective *makarioi*. The repetitious use of *makarioi* highlights the Beatitudes as a micro-discourse amongst a much larger discourse because the statements are the only ones of their kind in the entirety of the Sermon on the Mount. *Makarioi* is the predicate adjective of each verb in the Beatitudes. Each use of

17. Black, *It's Still Greek to Me*, 130.
18. Campbell, *Study of Greek*, 157.

Literary Features and Context

makarioi acts as a componential tie, namely that of co-classification describing "cohesive ties between linguistic items of the same class or genus."[19] In the case of Matt 5:3, those classified as *makarioi* are the same as those who are poor in spirit. The repeated use of the word *makarioi* as a co-classification creates a reference chain which Campbell describes as a chain that "creates cohesion by creating links between elements in a text."[20] The frequent use of *makarioi* creates an identity chain due to it being expressed by co-classification ties. Therefore, the Beatitudes are connected by the repetitious use of the predicate adjective. The predicate adjective in each Beatitude also acts as a boundary marker that begins and ends the series of statements presented within Matt 5:3–12 in that these statements are the only ones of their kind in the Sermon on the Mount.

The Beatitudes, although finding their background in wisdom literature,[21] also act as indicative statements providing a reality to believers that they can rest in presently. Matthew 5:3 gives assurance to the believer that they can live in a state of *makarioi* because they don't have to wait for the kingdom of heaven to be theirs—it is theirs already. The use of the present active indicative verb *estin* in Matt 5:3 provides a promise that is not future but is current in the lives of the believers, namely that they are already a part of the kingdom of heaven. The consistent use of *hoti* at the beginning of each subordinate clause explains why believers should live in a state of flourishing in a fallen world. Thankfully, Jesus does not just indicate that believers are *makarioi* but explains the cause of their flourishing. The Beatitudes not only profile believers as those who are *makarioi* but also provide hope for believers because of the promises indicated at the end of each statement. As a profile of believers, the Beatitudes connect wonderfully with the rest of the Sermon on the Mount, which guides those believers in holy living. There are many, however, who do not recognize the Beatitudes' separate function and purpose from the remainder of the Sermon on the Mount. Many different views blend the Beatitudes with the

---

19. Campbell, *Study of Greek*, 158.
20. Campbell, *Study of Greek*, 155.
21. Longman and Garland, *Matthew*, 159.

Section One: A Correct View of *Makarios* Leads to a Correct View

remainder of the Sermon on the Mount, treating them as wisdom literature that provides directions to enter the kingdom of God and be blessed.

4

Alternate Views of the Beatitudes

ACHIEVING A STATE OF morality that results in blessings from God is often seen as the foundation of interpreting the Beatitudes. According to Danny Akin, president of Southeastern Baptist Theological Seminary, there are eight different interpretative approaches to the Sermon on the Mount.[1] One interpretation is called the "Utopian Ideal Ethic," which states that the teaching provided in the Sermon on the Mount is impossible and unrealistic.[2] A second interpretation, called "Millennial Ethics," is that the Sermon on the Mount's teachings applies only to a future kingdom.[3] Thirdly, the "Spiritual Elite Ethic" says that the teaching within Christ's sermon is only for the truly spiritual.[4] A fourth interpretation, called the "Eschatological Ethic," states that Jesus gives principles just for the pending end-time period.[5] Another interpretation, called "Call to Repentance," states that the only intention of the sermon was to call people to repentance.[6] Another view concerning the Be-

1. Akin et al., *Exalting Jesus*, 14.
2. Akin et al., *Exalting Jesus*, 15.
3. Akin et al., *Exalting Jesus*, 15.
4. Akin et al., *Exalting Jesus*, 15.
5. Akin et al., *Exalting Jesus*, 15.
6. Akin et al., *Exalting Jesus*, 14.

Section One: A Correct View of *Makarios* Leads to a Correct View

atitudes called "The Principles of Life for Kingdom Citizens" states that the conduct of Jesus's followers is presented within the sermon as guidelines for any age.[7] Akin states there is an interpretation called the "Intentional/Internal Ethic" which states "one's intention and motivation is the thrust of the sermon."[8] Lastly, Akin presents an interpretation he agrees with called "A Perfect Standard for the Christian's Life," which says the Sermon on the Mount describes the lifestyle of those who belong to the kingdom of God.[9] Akin's last interpretation contrasts with the dominant alternate interpretation of the Beatitudes. The dominant alternate interpretation is a blend of the previous seven interpretations that Akin presents us with, known by Scot McKnight as "God's Favor," which states that the Beatitudes are a list of standards that, if performed correctly, will result in God's blessings. Understanding the Beatitudes as a list of standards that leads to God's favor leads to a man-centered theology that bases one's happiness and salvation on moral achievement. Since the God's Favor interpretation leads to a man-centered theology, it cheapens the work of Christ on the cross by claiming that man in his own strength can bring about God's bestowed blessings rather than receiving it by grace alone which breeds genuine happiness.

---

7. Akin et al., *Exalting Jesus*, 14.

8. Akin et al., *Exalting Jesus*, 14. According to Akin, Augustine agrees with the last two views presented above regarding the Sermon on the Mount, which can be seen in his sermon called "A Perfect Standard of Christian Living." Akin et al., *Exalting Jesus*, 16.

9. Akin et al., *Exalting Jesus*, 16. Sinclair Ferguson claims in his introductory sermon on the Sermon on the Mount, "The sermon is a description of the lifestyle of those who belong to the kingdom." Akin et al., *Exalting Jesus*, 16. According to Akin, Ferguson agrees with viewing the Beatitudes as "Principles of Life for Kingdom Living," based on his sermon statement. Akin et al., *Exalting Jesus*, 16. For a fuller explanation of Ferguson's view on the Beatitudes, see his commentary, *The Sermon on the Mount: Kingdom Life in a Fallen World*.

Alternate Views of the Beatitudes

Other Interpretations of the Sermon on the Mount

Like Akin, Scot McKnight provides three interpretations of the Sermon on the Mount that revolve around interpreting the Beatitudes as a list of standards that, if achieved, will guarantee God's blessings. Scot McKnight, professor of New Testament at Northern Baptist Theological Seminary, gives three interpretations that involve viewing the Beatitudes as qualities to achieve. His three interpretations are as follows: "Ethics from Above," which is morality based on commandments of the law; "Ethics from Beyond," which is morality based on the coming kingdom presented in the Prophets; and "Ethics from Below," which is morality based on wisdom, as seen in wisdom literature.[10] Although all three of these moralities are present in Christ's teachings within the Sermon on the Mount, the reasoning behind their attainment is where the most error occurs.

All three views are at play when interpreting the Beatitudes as morality standards that, if achieved, result in God's blessings. McKnight presents an alternate view called "God's Favor," which is incorrect due to misinterpreting the word "blessed" at the beginning of each Beatitude.[11] This misinterpretation of the word "blessed" will be discussed in the chapter of section one called "Interpreting the Word 'Blessed' and *Makarios*." Other commentators hold to McKnight's view that the Beatitudes are simply moral standards that will result in God's favor or blessings. These commentators validate McKnight's alternate interpretation by misinterpreting the Greek word *makarios*. David Turner, for instance, in his commentary on Matthew, states, "The Beatitudes reveal key character traits that God approves of in his people. Those who repent receive these character traits in principle but must cultivate them in the process of discipleship."[12] Turner's statement of the Beatitudes being key character traits that God approves of in his people may lead some people to believe that each of the nine Beatitudes is a specific

---

10. McKnight and Longman, *Sermon on the Mount*, 32.
11. McKnight and Longman, *Sermon on the Mount*, 32.
12. Turner, *Matthew*, 147.

trait that must be carried out to receive God's favor. This view of God's favor being placed on those who carry out each Beatitude is strengthened with the misinterpretation and mistranslation of the Greek word *makarios*, which, based on English translations, means "blessed." Reading the word "blessed" before each trait given specifically within a Beatitude shows that the trait presented, if acted upon, will result in being blessed by God. Some Greek philosophies confirm that being blessed is only achieved through means of development or following guidelines to achieve a blessing from the gods.[13]

Commentators Who Disagree with Alternate Interpretations of the Beatitudes

Several commentators disagree with these misinterpretations of the Beatitudes that result in God's favor including Sinclair Ferguson, Jonathan Pennington, Robert Guelich, and William Tyndale. William Tyndale says in his commentary on the Sermon on the Mount,

> All these deeds here rehearsed, as to nourish peace, to shew mercy, to suffer persecution, and so forth, make not a man happy and blessed; neither deserveth he reward of heaven; but declare and testify that we are happy and blessed, and that we shall have great promotion in heaven; and certify us in our breasts that we are God's sons, and that the Holy Ghost is in us: for all good things are given to us freely of God, for Christ's blood sake and his merits.[14]

William Tyndale, who was the first to translate the English Bible from the original languages, understood the error of interpreting the Beatitudes as a list of simple morality statements; this understanding was due to his understanding of the original languages. Tyndale, like Guelich, views the Beatitudes as a state of

---

13. McMahon, *Pursuit of Happiness*, 254.
14. Tyndale, *Expositions*, 228.

Alternate Views of the Beatitudes

blessedness or prosperity that results from an act of God alone and not based on man's merit.

In his book *The Divine Conspiracy*, Dallas Willard, a specialist in metaphysics, states, "The Beatitudes are not teachings on how to be blessed. They are not instructions to do anything. They do not indicate conditions that are especially pleasing to God or good for human beings."[15] Dallas has a future focus in mind when comparing the state of man in the Beatitudes to the state of man presented within the future, restored kingdom of God. All of these commentators have a similar understanding that the Beatitudes are not merits to perform to receive God's bestowed blessings but rather the state of a man who is in right relationship with God.

A term used to describe someone who is in a mature and intimate relationship with God is the Greek word *teleios*. *Teleios* is a term frequently used within the Sermon on the Mount, which is often diluted by the English gloss "perfect." Specifically within the Sermon on the Mount, Christ says in Matt 5:48, "Be ye perfect, even as your father which is in heaven is perfect;" this word for "perfect" is the Greek word *teleios*, which means "perfect, entire, or complete."[16] *Teleios* does not mean someone has to be perfect in following every aspect of God's law but rather that a person's wholeness or whole being is established in a deeply rooted relationship with God; thus, that person is in a true state of happiness as presented in the Beatitudes when they are made whole in Christ. The proper understanding of the word "blessed" or the Greek words *makarios* and *teleios* will give the appropriate view of the Beatitudes and refute the view of the Beatitudes as merit statements that lead to God's bestowed favor.

---

15. Willard, *Divine Conspiracy*, 99.
16. Liddell, *Greek-English Lexicon*, 1769.

5

Interpreting the Word "Blessed" and *Makarios*

A PROPER UNDERSTANDING OF the word "blessed" will not only refute the God's Favor view that Scot McKnight holds, as mentioned above which stems from a blend of both Second Temple Jewish and Greco-Roman contexts, but will solidify that the Beatitudes describe a state of fortune within those who follow Christ with wholeness of heart. The Beatitudes describe a state of fortune, a state of bliss, a state of true happiness desired by many. Some English translations have attempted to capture the meaning of the Greek word *makarios* with the English word "blessed" or the English word "happy." However, both provide a problem that confuses the interpretation of the Beatitudes and the remainder of the Sermon on the Mount.

In his book *Kingdom Living Here and Now*, John MacArthur, pastor and teacher at Grace Community Church, states that "our word 'blessed' comes from the Greek word *makarios*, an adjective that means happy or blissful."[1] Even though the words "happy" and "blissful," according to MacArthur, are weaker English words

---

1. MacArthur, *Kingdom Living*, 25.

for *makarios*, they still provide separation from the misleading English word "blessed." Where "blessed" denotes God's favor, "happy" or "blissful" correctly present a state of being, which is what *makarios* attempts to describe. Examining how *makarios* is used within the Greek Septuagint, extra-biblical writings, and amongst the early church fathers will validate its proper use within the New Testament. Understanding which Hebrew word within the Old Testament that *makarios* is used to translate into Greek is crucial in adequately interpreting the word's use in the Beatitudes. Hebrew words *'asrê* or *bārûk* can be confusing in their interpretation when glossed over with the English word "blessed," much like *makarios*. However, *makarios* is used only to translate one of these Hebrew words, which proves its proper use as describing a state of being rather than a bestowed blessing. Both *'asrê* and *bārûk* are translated into "blessed" within the Old Testament; however, *'asrê* reveals a state of human flourishing or true happiness while *bārûk* describes God's bestowed blessing.

The Use of *Makarios* and *'Asrê*

Each of the nine Beatitudes begins with the Greek word *makarios*. However, this is not the only place this Greek word is used throughout Matthew or the remaining Scripture. Many English translations have used different words to transition this Greek word into English. Some English translations have used words like "happy," "blissful," "fortunate," or "flourishing." However, interestingly, most literal translations, such as the New King James Version and the English Standard Version, stick with the word "blessed" as their English gloss. The English word "blessed" is used even within these literal translations and seems to be based on tradition.

The title in many subheadings of English Bibles labels the section of Matt 5:3–11 as the "Beatitudes" or "blessings" reflecting traditional thought. This label leads to confusion of interpretation, assuming that the following verses are to be read as blessings based on the condition or attitude given within the verses to be obtained. According to Pennington, a more technical term for "Beatitude"

Section One: A Correct View of *Makarios* Leads to a Correct View

is *macarism*.² *Macarism* is a *makarios* statement that does not describe a bestowed blessing or bestowed favor but ascribes happiness or flourishing to a particular person or state. Pennington rightly refutes that *macarism* means a bestowed blessing when he claims that *macarism* "is a pronouncement, based on observation, that a certain way of being in the world produces human flourishing and true happiness."³ The word *makarios* is used throughout much Jewish literature in their Greek translations, particularly in the Greek Septuagint, usually describing a state of tranquility.

In the Greek Septuagint, whenever the Hebrew word *'asrê* appears, it is translated into Greek as *makarios*. A simple word study of *makarios*'s use in the Septuagint will show that it is only used to translate the Hebrew term *'asrê*, never *bārûk*. Examining the root of *'asrê* validates *makarios* as a proper Greek gloss of the word. The root of *'asrê* is *'ir*. Aaron Ruben, professor of linguistics at Pennsylvania State University, claims in his article "The Form and Meaning of Hebrew *'Asrê*" that

> from the root *'ir* for which there are no obvious Semitic cognates, there also exists a *pi 'el* verb meaning 'praise, call happy,' which occurs about a dozen times throughout the Bible, and a noun *'asrê*, which only occurs once in the Bible within Genesis 30:13, but is well attested in post-biblical Hebrew, thus the root of *'asrê* fits with the traditional rendering of the Hebrew word *'asrê* as happy.⁴

Secular use of the word seems to give the idea of lucky or fortunate; however, within Scripture, the meaning of *'asrê* goes much deeper by placing an emphasis on the condition of man in the right relationship with God.⁵ Thus, the person in the right relationship with God—namely, a covenantal relationship—is rendered *'asrê*, or truly fortunate or truly happy. Extra-biblical commentary shows Rabbinic usage of *'asrê* "follows the pattern of its use in the Psalms and

---

2. Pennington, *Human Flourishing*, 42.
3. Pennington, *Human Flourishing*, 42.
4. Ruben, "Form and Meaning," 366–72.
5. Gemeren, *New International Dictionary*, 570–72.

Proverbs, in particular the wisdom emphasis on the truly happy state of the Torah-keeping life."[6]

Other languages such as Arabic and Akkadian also suggest, like the Hebrew, that the root of the word *'asrê* points toward its use to describe a state of human flourishing or fortune. Rubin validates this when he says, "Given the range of meanings for this root in Arabic, Akkadian, and Hebrew, it is reasonable to assume that Proto-Semitic *sry/srw* meant something like 'well-off, prosperous.' Whatever the original meaning of the root *sry* in Proto-Semitic, it came to mean something like 'happy' in Hebrew, a natural semantic shift."[7] The root of *'asrê* rules out the use of the English gloss "blessed" and validates the use of the English gloss "flourishing" or "fortunate."

The idea of human flourishing is presented through the Hebrew word *'asrê*, with the goal of reaching a state of *shalom*. The word *shalom* is usually glossed over in English to mean "peace," again providing a watered-down version of what the Hebrew is trying to accomplish. To many, the word "peace" means an absence of war or conflict. *Shalom*, however, means assurance, an inner peace that stems from a covenantal relationship with God.[8] The state of *shalom* is thus connected with the idea of flourishing or true inner happiness that the Hebrew word *'asrê* means. The Hebrew *'asrê* is a noun that always occurs as a construct intensive.[9] According to Pennington, since the Hebrew word *'asrê* is always a construct intensive, it is "followed by and connected with the who being described as *'asrê*; *'asrê* is the one who is in a state of happiness."[10] Therefore, if the Beatitudes were translated into Hebrew, it would read like "*'asrê* is the poor in spirit," showing that those who are "poor in spirit" are those who are living in a state of fortune or flourishing.

6. Brown, "אָשֵׁר," 1:571; paraphrased from Pennington, *Human Flourishing*, 88.
7. Ruben, *Form and Meaning*, 366–72.
8. Bryan, "Discourse on Human Flourishing."
9. Freedman et al., *Anchor Bible Dictionary*, 629–31.
10. Pennington, *Human Flourishing*, 44.

Section One: A Correct View of *Makarios* Leads to a Correct View

Makarios/'Asrê Use in the Psalms

Twenty-six of the forty-five occurrences of the word *'asrê* are found in the psalms, eight in the proverbs, and the other remaining occurrences dispersed throughout Scripture. Each occurrence describes not a bestowed blessing upon someone from God but rather a state of *shalom*, or a state of human flourishing. Psalm 1 is a popular psalm that begins within the Greek Septuagint with the word *makarios*. The Hebrew word at the beginning of Ps 1 is the word *'asrê*. The English gloss weakens and confuses the running thought throughout the psalm by translating *makarios* or *'asrê* into the English word "blessed." As within the Beatitudes, the confusion seems to draw the idea that if someone performs the actions presented within Ps 1, that person will be blessed. However, Pennington's translation captures the meaning behind the word *'asrê* or *makarios* well by using the translation "flourishing is the man" for Ps 1:1.[11] Pennington's translation shows that the description of the man presented in Ps 1 is a man flourishing or in a true state of *shalom*, which is seen in the description of him being "like a tree planted by the rivers of water" (V3a).

When thinking like a Second Temple Jew who uses the directions given in wisdom literature to be blessed, one could misinterpret the blessing presented at the beginning of Ps 1 as one that is only obtained through the directions given in the remaining verses. Viewing Ps 1 through such a lens may lead to legalism, just as it does when interpreting the Beatitudes through the same lens alone. In her book *God and the Art of Happiness*, Ellen Charry refutes that this psalm is a list of requirements to be blessed by, concluding that the psalms do not push adherence to "Pentateuchal legislation."[12] In other words, the psalms do not present a list of demands to follow to receive God's blessings, creating a merit-based reward system. This confusion leads to the dangerous notion that a person's works as given in the requirements of Scripture plus God's grace lead to blessings and salvation.

---

11. Pennington, *Human Flourishing*, 44.
12. Charry, *God and the Art of Happiness*, 214.

Interpreting the Word "Blessed" and Makarios

In other places within the psalms, the lemma 'asrê is found seventeen times. Psalms 40:4, 65:4, and many others have the lemma present, being denoted as a state of extended happiness or fortune. In Ps 40:4, the lemma 'asrê occurs and is translated with the English gloss "blessed"; however, scholars of Lexham's Faithlife Study Bible understand that the word "blessed" is not an adequate gloss of the lemma. Lexham's Faithlife Study Bible states concerning 'asrê in Ps 40:4, "The Hebrew word *ashre* ('happy' or 'blessed') is a common expression to indicate that someone is fortunate or privileged."[13] Lexham's more detailed explanation on the word 'asrê is found in their notes regarding Ps 1:1, saying, "Wisdom Literature commonly uses this expression to indicate someone who is fortunate or privileged (Job 5:17; Pr 3:13; 28:14). Its Greek equivalent—*Makarios*—is found in Jesus's beatitudes (Matt 5:3–11)."[14] Based on Lexham's study notes concerning the word 'asrê, a more adequate English translation of Ps 40:4 would be "Fortunate or privileged is the man who makes the LORD his trust." Thus, the most basic form of the word 'asrê denotes a state of fortune rather than a bestowed blessing.

Makarios/'Asrê Use in Proverbs

Another place where the word 'asrê is frequently used is within the proverbs. For example, Prov 8:32 states using the word 'asrê, "Now therefore hearken unto me, O ye children: for blessed are they that keep my ways." The Hebrew word 'asrê is again translated into "blessed" within this proverb; it is also a textbook example of how the word 'asrê is usually followed by the phrase "are those." Here, the term "blessed" also implies that those who do what is listed within the verse will have a bestowed blessing upon them. However, the Greek Septuagint recognizes the use of the Hebrew word 'asrê and translates it over into *makarios*, meaning "flourishing" or "fortunate." Proverbs 8:32 thus says, "Now therefore hearken

---

13. *Faithlife Study Bible*, Ps 40:4.
14. *Faithlife Study Bible*, Ps 1:1.

unto me, O ye children: for flourishing or happy are they that keep my ways." A state of blessing, a state of flourishing, and *shalom* is presented as the one who keeps the way of the Lord.

Another place in Proverbs where the word *'asrê* or the Greek word *makarios* is used is in Prov 14:21. In most English translations of this verse, the last few words are "blessed is he." Again, the English gloss of the word *'asrê* is rendered "blessed," which may lead to the confusion that God will bless you if you are generous to the poor. The word *'asrê* in this proverb describes a happy/flourishing state of the man or woman who is generous to the poor. The glossing of the word *'asrê* in Prov 14:21 with the word "blessed" can lead to a social-justice view of Scripture, claiming that this proverb commands us to be generous to the poor to receive God's favor. *'Asrê* is also found in Prov 3:13. According to the translators of the NET Bible regarding the usage of the lemma within Prov 3:13, "This word reflects that inner joy and heavenly bliss which comes to the person who is pleasing to God, whose way is right before God."[15] Thus it is clear that *'asrê* describes much more than a simple blessing but a life that is completely changed by God to a state of blissfulness. Therefore, *makarios* being used as a gloss in the Septuagint version of Proverbs must mean that its use in the New Testament also denotes a state of bliss that a person obtains from God.

Use of *'Asrê* Elsewhere

The word *'asrê* is also found in Job 5:17, where Job says, "Behold, happy is the man whom God correcteth." Here the KJV gets the gloss closer to the original meaning of the word *'asrê*, while most English translations translate *'asrê* as "blessed." However, based on the context, the use of the translation "happy" describes a long-term state of being rather than a single event. Job has experienced loss to the extent that will change his life and lifestyle moving forward, thus Job's friend sees Job's suffering as God's reproof.

---

15. Biblical Studies Press, *NET Bible First Edition Notes*, Prov 3:13.

Interpreting the Word "Blessed" and Makarios

According to Job's friend, such reproach is God's way of bringing Job to a deeper relationship with the Almighty which in turn will provide a more fortunate life. 'Asrê does occur in Isaiah where the word is used twice, similar to its use in the psalms. Notice how the English Standard Version recognizes that the word 'asrê means a state of flourishing rather than a bestowed blessing; in the ESV, Isa 32:20 reads, "Happy are you who sow beside all waters, who let the feet of the ox and the donkey range free." The word 'asrê or *makarios*, depending on if one is translating from the original Hebrew or the Greek Septuagint, is translated here by the English gloss "happy." Again, Isa 32:30 further proves that the word 'asrê reveals a state of happiness or flourishing rather than as bestowed or given as a blessing from God. Pennington describes what is taking place within Isaiah well when he says,

> In Isaiah 30:18, there is the proclaiming of the happy state of the person who, even in the midst of suffering, waits upon and trusts in the Lord; second in Isaiah 32:20 proclaiming the happy state of those who will live and flourish under the coming king who will reign in righteousness, the very context where *shalom* also occurs with great import.[16]

Pennington's review of the use of 'asrê in both Isa 30:18 and 32:20 proves that *shalom* and 'asrê go hand in hand when describing a state of being.

Makarios and the New Testament

Makarios is used some fifty times within the New Testament, denoting a state of fortune or bliss. The word often depicts the same idea of its Hebrew equivalent 'asrê. Pennington rightly points out that "when one considers the dual context of Second Temple Judaism and Greco-Roman influence, we see how the 'asrê and *shalom* tradition of human flourishing continues."[17] Each time the word

---

16. Pennington, *Human Flourishing*, 45.
17. Pennington, *Human Flourishing*, 46.

makarios is presented within the New Testament, it continues the thought and feel of the Old Testament word *'asrê*. Therefore, as Pennington states, "This striking correspondence gives us a great reason to believe that the Greek Bible's *makarios* communicates the same idea of human flourishing and well-being as *'asrê*."[18]

An example of Scripture outside of Matthew's Gospel that uses the word *makarios* can be found in John's Gospel, specifically in John 20:29, where Jesus tells Thomas, "Because thou hast seen me, thou hast believed: blessed are they that have not seen, and yet have believed." The word "blessed" within the context here denotes one who is in a state of true inner happiness due to believing in Christ. Paul even describes a state of true inner happiness or, according to the English gloss, "happier" in 1 Cor 7:40. Paul states, "But she is happier if she so abide, after my judgment." The Greek word *makarios* in 1 Cor 7:40 is translated into "happier" rather than "blessed," again denoting a state of being rather than a bestowed blessing from God.

Makarios in Matthew's Gospel

The use of *makarios* within Matthew is seen in Matt 5:3–11 in the giving of the Beatitudes and other areas of Matthew's Gospel. The different areas in which *makarios* is presented provide validation that the correct use of *makarios* describes a state of being rather than a bestowed blessing by God. Each time *makarios* is used within Matthew's Gospel, it remains glossed over with the English word "blessed." Outside of the Beatitudes presented in Matt 5, there are four other occurrences of *makarios*.

In Matt 11, Christ begins to travel around to preach repentance and the coming kingdom. John the Baptist is in prison during this time and, while in prison, he sends out his disciples to check if Jesus is the messiah that they have been waiting for. Jesus responds to John's disciples by confirming who he is by telling them all the works and signs that he has performed. He then says in verse 16

---

18. Pennington, *Human Flourishing*, 44.

that the one who welcomes his coming will be *makarios*, finding themselves in a state of bliss and eternal happiness while the others will have woes placed upon them. Jesus says that the one who does not accept him will live in dissatisfaction, while the one who does accept him will live in a state of blissfulness.

Another occurrence of *makarios* in seen in Matt 13:16, where Jesus says, "But blessed are your eyes, for they see, and your ears, for they hear." Jesus is contrasting in this verse those whose eyes were open to see that he is the Christ with those whose eyes remained blind to who Christ is. Those whose eyes are open to Christ, spiritually understanding that he is the Son of God, are *makarios*, or in a state of true flourishing. Those who do not see spiritually that Christ is the Son of God live in the opposite state of flourishing; they are in agony and constantly longing to see Christ but can't (Matt 13:17).

Another use of *makarios* outside of the Beatitudes is seen in Matt 16:17, where Christ says to Peter, "Blessed art thou, Simon Bar-Jonah: For flesh and blood hath not revealed it unto thee, but my Father which is in heaven." The use of *makarios* here describes that Peter is in is in a convenutal relationship with God due to God revealing who Christ is to him, resulting in a present and future state of eternal flourishing. This verse also proves that, ultimately, man cannot achieve *makarios*, but God gives *makarios* through revealing and drawing his elect to himself. When God chooses to reveal his Christ to a person, that one comes becomes *makarios*. Pennington agrees when stating, "The context is the discussion of God revealing himself to people so that they are able to understand because mere human faculties are incapable of comprehending and receiving the mysterious realities of God."[19] Christ confirms that Peter is not receiving a blessing from God for doing something, but Peter is in a state of *makarios* due to God revealing himself to him.

The last use of *makarios* outside of the Beatitudes is seen in Matt 24:46, where Jesus says, "Blessed is that servant whom his lord when he cometh shall find so doing." It is the good and wise

---

19. Pennington, *Human Flourishing*, 56.

servant within this parable that is described as *makarios*. According to the parable that Jesus presents within Matt 24:36–51, those who are found serving God when Christ returns are those who are *makarios*. While this service seems to be founded in human effort, it stems from God who implants a heart in his elect to serve him. One does not just begin serving God without God first doing a work within them. Humankind's depraved nature will not allow them to first serve God before God has drawn them to himself. Therefore, the servant's efforts within this parable stem from a new heart that God has caused to be born within him. The use of *makarios* throughout Matthew and the remainder of the New Testament solidifies its meaning as a state of being rather than a bestowed blessing from God towards man.

Makarios Outside of the Canon

The culture that surrounded the Sermon on the Mount was heavily Greek-influenced, yet still the Aramaic language was prominent. The common language of Judea around the first century AD was most likely Aramaic.[20] The villages of Nazareth and Capernaum in Galilee, where Christ spent most of his ministry, were Aramaic-speaking communities that had enough Greek influence that most people could also understand and speak koine Greek.[21] The Greek language had been spread throughout the world of Christ, and many philosophers of his day and Paul's day spoke fluent Greek, using the term *makarios* in some of their writings. MacArthur states, "The Greeks called the island of Cyprus the happy isle," using the word *makarios* to describe the state of the island.[22]

The ancient Greek philosopher Aristotle uses the word *makarios* in his book *Nicomachean Ethics*; the word translates into English as "supreme happiness." In *Nicomachean Ethics*, Aristotle says, "And there are some external goods the absence of which

---

20. "Jesus and the Apostles," *Britannica*.
21. Wright, *Interpreting Jesus*, 35.
22. MacArthur, *Kingdom Living*, 25.

Interpreting the Word "Blessed" and Makarios

spoils supreme happiness, e.g., good birth, good children, and beauty: for a man who is very ugly in appearance or ill-born or who lives all by himself and has no children cannot be classified as altogether happy; even less happy perhaps is a man whose children and friends are worthless, or one who has lost good children and friends through death."[23] In each English translation of Aristotle's work, the word *makarios* is rendered "happy." Like many ancient Greek philosophers, Aristotle's use of *makarios* describes a state of being rather than a merit-based blessing.

Again, the use of *makarios* is not just subject to Scripture; other literature also validates its use as describing a state of being rather than a bestowed blessing. In Greek poetry outside of Scripture, *makarios* described the condition of the gods and those who share their happy existence.[24] The frequent use of the word *makarios* in poetry and Scripture during the Greco-Roman era allowed it to become a common term used by people to describe themselves as "happy" or "blissful." According to *The NIV Theological Dictionary of New Testament Words*, *makarios* describes "people who were congratulated on happy events, such as parents on their children, the rich on their wealth, the wise on their knowledge, the pious on their inward well-being, and initiates their experience of God."[25]

Other extra-biblical literature, such as *The Odyssey* by Homer, uses the word *makarios* to inform an individual's state of being. In his book *A Study of the Semantic Field Denoting Happiness in Ancient Greek to the End of the 5th Century B.C.*, Cornelis de Heer claims regarding the use of *makarios* in *The Odyssey* that "to be *makar* (*makarios*) is to be divine, to have a home secure against adversity, to be untroubled by wind and rain, to enjoy perpetual sunshine, enjoy oneself all day long." According to Heer, the use of *makarios* in *The Odyssey* portrays a state of enjoyment or happiness and not something that is given but felt within the person.[26]

23. Aristotle, *Nicomachean Ethics* 1101a 1–10.
24. Verbrugge, *NIV Theological Dictionary*, 352.
25. Verbrugge, *NIV Theological Dictionary*, 352.
26. Heer, *Study of the Semantic Field*, 4.

Makarios is also seen in some of the works of the apostolic fathers such as 1 Clem. The English translation of 1 Clem. 44:5 says, "Blessed [*makarios*] are those presbyters who died beforehand, who have obtained a fruitful and perfect departure, for they have no fear, lest anyone remove them from their established place."[27] Clement is stating that those who have died and are liberated from their flesh are now flourishing in a heavenly state of being with Christ. There seems to be a soteriological focus for those who have died in Christ mentioned in this verse, namely that those who died in Christ are considered blessed when they depart from this world and into the next. Describing Christ as a gate that leads to a blessed life, Clement states that those who enter Christ and "direct their course in holiness and righteousness, accomplishing everything without confusion" are the ones who are blessed.[28] Many others outside of the canon of Scripture like Josephus and Philo use the word *makarios*, describing a state of being for those who are in Christ.

Woes and Curses

In the New Testament, Luke also uses the word *makarios* when presenting his account of Christ's Sermon on the Mount. Luke's Gospel presents Christ's Sermon on the Mount in a different order than Matthew, proving that word *makarios* is rendered better as a state of being rather than God's bestowed blessings due to the series of woes that immediately follow. Luke provides us with his account of Jesus's Sermon on the Mount in chapter 6 of his Gospel. However, unlike Matthew, who saves the woes for the middle and end of the sermon, Luke presents the woes immediately after the Beatitudes to draw contrasts between two different states of being. Woes are not curses but denote the opposite in state of being rather than the opposite of God's bestowed blessing.

The opposite of a blessing is a curse, while the opposite of happiness is a state of mourning or sadness, which is considered

27. 1 Clem. 48:4.
28. 1 Clem. 48:4

Interpreting the Word "Blessed" and Makarios

a woe. According to Pennington, *macarisms* and woes are "invitations to living based on sapiential reflections, not divine speech of reward and cursings."[29] The distinction between the Hebrew words *bārûk* and *'asrê* is seen in their antonyms, the opposite of *'asrê* being a woe and the opposite of *bārûk* being a curse. Whenever the word *makarios* is presented in Luke's version of the Beatitudes, he does not follow up with a series of curses but rather a series of woes. According to Luke 6:20, Jesus says, "Blessed be ye poor, for yours is the kingdom of God," while following with "woe" statements that give the opposite idea of being in a state of happiness. Jesus would provide the opposite of being in a state of bliss in Luke 6:24, saying, "But woe to you who are rich! for ye have received your consolation." In other words, the poor are in a true state of flourishing or blissfulness, resulting in obtaining the kingdom of God, while the rich are in a temporal state of flourishing which will end in a state far worse than their current condition. Pennington establishes well that *makarios* is a state of being rather than a blessing bestowed by contrasting a woe from a curse. Pennington says, "A woe is the opposite of a *macarism* in that it describes the result of a way of being in the world that does not result in flourishing but in loss, grief, and destruction."[30]

While a woe corresponds with *'asrê* not only in the Old Testament but within the translation of *makarios* in the New Testament, cursings correspond with *bārûk*, or blessings being bestowed within the Old Testament. *'Asrê* and *makarios* are about human flourishing, while another word that is glossed over in the English with the word "blessed" (*bārûk*) gives the connotation of God's bestowed favor. The English gloss of "blessed" is translated for both Hebrew words that confuse the rendering of the Beatitudes. As stated above, *makarios* and the Hebrew word *'asrê* mean "human flourishing." The Greek Septuagint recognizes this by rendering *'asrê* as *makarios* while never rendering *bārûk* as *makarios*. The following section will provide an exegesis of the Hebrew word *bārûk* to show its difference in meaning from *'asrê*.

29. Pennington, *Human Flourishing*, 44.
30. Pennington, *Human Flourishing*, 53.

6

Bārûḵ vs. *'Asrê*

ALTHOUGH GLOSSED OVER WITH the same English word "blessed," *bārûḵ* means "God's favor bestowed" rather than "the flourishing state of being" that the Hebrew word *'asrê* means. Confusion has been caused by the English translations of both *'asrê* and *bārûḵ* as "blessed." The double use of the English gloss "blessed" leads many to believe that the Beatitudes represent a list of demands one must accomplish to have God's blessing (or *bārûḵ*) bestowed upon you. As mentioned earlier, the Greek word used in the Beatitudes, *makarios*, is used as a translation for the word *'asrê* throughout the Old Testament, while not used for the word *bārûḵ*. This dissolves the argument that *makarios* means "God's blessings bestowed." The distinction between the word *bārûḵ* and *'asrê* will provide a foundation that will lead to a proper view of the Beatitudes.

Bārûḵ Interpretations

The Hebrew word *bārûḵ* has been interpreted in many ways. Christopher Wright Mitchell, a graduate of Concordia Seminary, states in his book *The Meaning of* Bārûḵ "that different views of interpreting *bārûḵ* came about by three questions: First, what does

Bārûk vs. 'Asrê

blessing consist of? Second, what is the purpose of blessing? And third, how does blessing operate?"[1] Views by scholars such as Jahanned Pedersen show that *bārûk* meant that God's blessing was not just on the body of man, but God bestowed his favor on the soul of man as well.[2] Mitchell shows that Pedersen defines blessings or *bārûk* as "the power which fills the soul, provides power and growth."[3] Mitchell shows, however, that Pedersen takes a mystic approach: "that God, through his *bārûk*, gives a small portion of his power to us as well."[4] A common and conservative interpretation of *bārûk* still shows without mystic factors that *bārûk* does mean God's bestowed favor. This interpretation is given by many conservative scholars, including Claus Westermann. Westermann believes that *bārûk* means that God blesses through continual activity in promoting a prosperous state of being, so *bārûk* is an activity from God towards man.[5] Westermann's interpretation feeds the hope that the Greco-Roman culture blended with the Second Temple Jewish culture had that if you are more moral by following wisdom literature, God will bless you with true flourishing. While Westermann is correct that *bārûk* does insinuate God's favor placed upon you that could lead to a flourishing state, *bārûk* is not always used this way in Scripture.

Common Uses of *Bārûk*

The word *bārûk* is significantly used in Scripture, dealing with God's bestowment of fertility, health, or prosperity.[6] *Bārûk* occurs 327 times as a verb throughout the Old Testament, 189 times meaning "to bless" resulting from God's favor, and 47 times meaning "to be blessed." The word is used another 43 times denoting a

1. Mitchell, *Meaning of BRK*, 17.
2. Mitchell, *Meaning of BRK*, 18.
3. Mitchell, *Meaning of BRK*, 18.
4. Mitchell, *Meaning of BRK*, 18.
5. Mitchell, *Meaning of BRK*, 17.
6. Alexander et al., *Dictionary of the Old Testament*, 83.

Section One: A Correct View of *Makarios* Leads to a Correct View

verbal blessing, 36 as a claim from a person's promise to be blessed, and used in 4 places in Job denoting a curse and the invoking of harm. In the Pentateuch alone, *bārûḵ* is found over 160 times, appearing most frequently within Genesis and Deuteronomy—over 130 times.[7] The NET Bible gives a great example of the common use of the word *bārûḵ* in its notes on Exod 18:10. The NET translators state in their notes on *bārûḵ*'s usage in Exod 18:10, "The verb בָּרוּךְ (*barukh*) is the Qal passive participle of the verb. Here must be supplied a jussive, making this participle the predicate: 'May Yahweh be blessed.'"[8] The NET translators continue, noting this verse by saying, "The verb essentially means 'to enrich'; in praise it would mean that he would be enriched by the praises of the people."[9] It seems each time within its occurrence that the thought is always God's bestowment of favor upon man after performing God's requirements, or at times (as in Exod 18:10) man's bestowment of verbal blessing to God.

Outside of Scripture, *bārûḵ* is found sparingly in pre-Christian Hebrew literature, only retained in each instance as "blessed." *Bārûḵ* is also found in the Qumran literature, which seems to have a particular meaning but still retains the aspect of being blessed to some extent. For example, in 1 QS 6:5, priests would pray over their food and say, "Speak the blessing over bread/wine, give thanks for bread/wine."[10] *Bārûḵ* is used in this example for the word "blessing" as a pronounced blessing over a materialistic object. The linguistic usage within the deuterocanonical books also confirms *bārûḵ*'s meaning as "blessed." In Tob 3:11; 8:5, 15; 11:14; and 13:8, *bārûḵ* is used with the expression "Blessed be . . ." The Old Testament's use of *bārûḵ* also confirms its meaning. Many within the Old Testament looked for God's favor concerning fertility or prosperity, and the word *bārûḵ* was used in this manner, but not always.

7. Alexander et al., *Dictionary of the Old Testament*, 83.
8. Biblical Studies, *NET Bible*, Exod 18:10.
9. Biblical Studies, *NET Bible*, Exod 18:10.
10. Botterweck and Ringgren, *Theological Dictionary of the Old Testament*, 301–2.

Bārûḵ vs. 'Asrê

The term *bārûḵ* is used not just for blessings from God concerning fertility, wealth, or dominion, but for God's general favor in all areas of life. The priestly blessing in Num 6 calls for God's general attitude of favor to be placed on the person receiving the blessings. Numbers 6:24–26 shows the extent of *bārûḵ* that God bestows upon his people, saying, "The LORD bless thee, and keep thee: the LORD make his face shine upon thee, and be gracious unto thee: The LORD lift up his countenance upon thee, and give thee peace." Patrick Miller, former Old Testament professor of theology at Princeton Seminary, says concerning Num 6:24–26, "All three verses commence with a general expression of God's favor and end with a request for a somewhat more concrete benefit; the initial phrase employing *bārûḵ* is the most general; it is an 'all-inclusive petition.'"[11] *Bārûḵ* is thus used differently than the word *'asrê* by representing God's general favor on humankind. *Bārûḵ* is often associated with the common Old Testament phrase "God's face shines upon them," which again denotes a bestowed blessing rather than a state of being that the individual is presented within. The English gloss "blessed" thus is appropriately used in bestowed blessing statements rather than statements concerning a state of fortune for humankind, such as in verse 1 of Ps 1.

Bārûḵ's use within the Old Testament differs from the use of *'asrê*, which again represents a flourishing state of an individual, mostly within greeting and farewell statements. Ruth contains a great example of a greeting that obtains the word *bārûḵ*. When Boaz returns to his field in chapter 2 of Ruth, his employees greet him, saying within verse 4, "The Lord bless thee." This English gloss of "bless" is correct in this case because the statement indicates a hopeful bestowed blessing from God rather than a state of being. Often, greetings and farewells within the Old Testament that contained the word *bārûḵ* could be spoken by both authorities and subordinates concerning the hope that God would bestow favor on the individual they were acknowledging.[12] Other times, *bārûḵ* is seen as a man giving praise to God as a "blessing."

11. Miller, "Blessing of God," 240–51.
12. Clements, "Segen im Alten Testament," 238–39.

Section One: A Correct View of *Makarios* Leads to a Correct View

Genesis 12:1–3 is a foundational passage promoting the theme of the Hebrew word *bārûk* as it is used throughout the Old Testament. In this passage, Yahweh says to Abraham, "Get thee out of thy country, and from they kindred and from thy father's house, unto a land that I will shew thee: and I will make of thee a great nation and I will bless [*bārûk*] thee, and make thy name great; and thou shalt be a blessing: and I will bless [*bārûk*] them that bless thee, and curse them that cruse thee." In this passage, a form of the word *bārûk* is used five times as a result of human action and obedience to God. Genesis 12:2 presents *bārûk* as a Piel verb serving a causative function. In other words, the cause of the blessing received by Abram is his leaving his Father's house as God commanded him. Its other uses in the beginning of Gen 12:3 also function as a causative, denoting that those who bless Abraham will be blessed and vice versa, and those that curse who Abraham will be cursed. In other cases, there is a cause and effect based on human action, thus blessing or cursing is the result of human effort. Therefore, it seems *bārûk* is something that is bestowed because of an action, while *'asrê* is never derived from an action but simply a description of a state of being. *'Asrê* is not preceded with a command, while *bārûk* is almost always preceded by a command to receive *bārûk*. Another difference between *'asrê* and *bārûk* is seen in what follows *bārûk* in this passage. God does not offer a series of woes to those who afflict Abraham but simply curses which does not denote a life of agony but rather a momentary or temporal consequence.

Within the Beatitudes, specifically in Luke's account, they are followed by a series of woes that are the antonym of the *macarisms* presented above them. As stated previously, woes are not curses; they differ in that woes denote an unfortunate state of being rather than a lack of God's bestowed blessing. The opposite of a blessing is a curse, while the opposite of a state of happiness is a state of mourning or sadness, thus a woe. There are three Hebrew roots that are associated with cursing. Most curses within the Old Testament are associated with *bārûk* rather than *'asrê*. The opposite of God's favor is to have God's favor taken away and a state of agony following. Another example of the relationship between cursing and blessing is seen in the story of Noah. Noah, like Abraham, had to be obedient and perform specific duties for God's favor to be bestowed upon him. The opposite of God's favor is seen in what happens to those outside of Noah's ark. Due to their disobedience, they were left to drown and die. Again, unlike ʿasrê, which is not presented with a list of duties as bārûk, bārûk is always a result of someone doing something or performing a certain act.

Five Themes of *Bārûk*

Scot McKnight gives five themes associated with *bārûk*. The first theme is a phrase that McKnight states means "the one who the God of Israel blesses."[13] This is seen where those who would follow the wisdom of Moses given in Deuteronomy received God's blessing as a result. Secondly, there is an "eschatological focus" on the word *bārûk*.[14] When God restores his kingdom on earth, all will be blessed in the future, as seen in the prophecies of Daniel and Isaiah. The third theme is "conditionality," meaning those who are *bārûk* are marked by specific attributes or characteristics.[15] Fourthly is what McKnight calls the theme of "relational disposition."[16] Relational disposition means that those who receive God's favor are in an obedient relationship with him.[17] Last is a theme called "reversal or contrast."[18] This theme states that God's favor is placed upon those least expected by society to have his favor. This last theme can be seen in the presentation of the Beatitudes: those who are "poor in spirit" have God's favor rather than the rich like society thought. However, this last theme is invalid regarding the Beatitudes because the Beatitudes' use of *makarios*

13. McKnight, *Sermon on the Mount*, 32.
14. McKnight, *Sermon on the Mount*, 32.
15. McKnight, *Sermon on the Mount*, 32.
16. McKnight, *Sermon on the Mount*, 32.
17. McKnight, *Sermon on the Mount*, 33.
18. McKnight, *Sermon on the Mount*, 32.

Section One: A Correct View of *Makarios* Leads to a Correct View

says that those who are "poor in spirit" are in a state of true happiness rather than receiving a bestowed blessing for being "poor in spirit." Each of the themes McKnight presents shows that *bārûk* is correctly interpreted as God's favor in both wisdom and prophetic literature. Never is *bārûk* related to a theme that describes a state of man; however, it may be used to describe the giving of that state. Therefore, the Beatitudes are appropriately interpreted through the lens of *'asrê* rather than *bārûk*. *'Asrê* describes a state of being rather than God's bestowed favor, as seen with *bārûk*.

R. T. France clarifies the distinction between *bārûk* and *'asrê/makarios* with his thoughts regarding their English gloss. According to France, *'asrê* is the "background to the macarisms," therefore "happy" is a better translation than "blessed."[19] He also states that while "happy" is not fully adequate, it is better than "blessed," which has too theological a connotation that God blesses those presented within the Beatitudes."[20] *Bārûk* is often presented as an active verb due to requirements by humanity that are given by God for them to meet. *'Asrê* or *makarios*, as presented within the Beatitudes, are not active verbs but rather descriptions of positions or states of being. *'Asrê*, unlike *bārûk*, is a result, however, not of requirements being met but a covenantal relationship with God that leads to a state of human flourishing. Next, interpreting the Greek word *teleios* as an intimate relationship with God will solidify the correct use of *makarios* as presented above.

---

19. France, *Gospel of Matthew*, 160–61.
20. France, *Gospel of Matthew*, 160–61.

7

Teleios and *Makarios*

THE GREEK TERM *TELEIOS* is related to achieving *makarios*, as presented within the Beatitudes. *Teleios*, like *makarios*, has been diluted by its English gloss presented throughout the New Testament. *Teleios* is often glossed over with the word "perfect," leading many to struggle to achieve what the modern world's definition of "perfect" portrays. The word *teleios* is seen within the command Jesus presents at the end of chapter 5 of Matthew's Gospel. Jesus uses the word *teleios* in Matt 5:48, saying, "Be ye therefore *perfect*, even as your Father which is in heaven is *perfect*." With this improper English gloss of "perfect" in the place of *teleios*, this commandment seems unachievable, and those who strive to be perfect like God will live a life of legalism hoping that God will bless them based on their merit. With this misleading English gloss, it is easy to tie the word "perfect" with the other English gloss "blessed" as presented within the Beatitudes to breed a legalistic mindset that blessing will be bestowed if perfection is achieved. However, the correct rendering of the Greek word *teleios* presents the opposite of moral achievement by describing a state of covenantal intimacy with God. If *teleios* is viewed as a state rather than a requirement, then the correct view of *makarios* emerges.

Section One: A Correct View of *Makarios* Leads to a Correct View

Teleios is used nineteen times as a Greek gloss for certain Hebrew words in the Old Testament. It is used several times as a gloss for *shalom*, *tamim*, and others. In most cases, it denotes within the Septuagint something being brought to completion or maturity. The word is seen as early as Gen 6:9, where it is used to describe Noah as blameless. Genesis 6:9 is not indicating that Noah was sinless but rather that Noah's life was devoted to following and obeying God while repenting of sin if necessary. In God's warning to his chosen nation Israel not to succumb to the practices of the nations around them, he commands Israel to remain blameless or *teleios*. In Solomon's benediction as he prays for Israel, he requests in 1 Kgs 8:61 that Israel "let [their] heart[s] therefore be perfect." Here the Septuagint uses another form of *teleios*, namely *teleia*, better rendered "mature" then "perfect." Two forms of *teleios* are found at the end of Jer 13:18 of the Greek Septuagint. The first form of *teleios* seen in this verse is *sunetelesen* written as an aorist active verb indicative which could be glossed with the English word "finished." Secondly, *teleios* appears as an adjective at the end of Jer 13:18, once again describing something that is "complete." In most cases, whether an adjective or verb, *teleios* seems to indicate something "completed" or "matured" in its entirety and not necessarily "perfect," meaning "sinless."

Classical Greek literature also confirms the use of *teleios* as completion and not mere perfection that one must achieve. According to Verbrugge, "The noun *telos* meant a turning point, the culminating point at which one state ends and another begins; later the goal, the end."[1] Classical Greek marks the use of *teleios* as a state of completing a goal, arriving at a climax, or being filled.[2] Greek philosophy within Greek literature also describes *teleios* as a state of completion. In Plato's and Aristotle's philosophies, "the *teleios* to which one aspires is an ethical goal and ultimately brings happiness and bliss."[3] Thus to be "complete" means to be "happy."

---

1. Verbrugge, *NIV Theological Dictionary*, 559.
2. Verbrugge, *NIV Theological Dictionary*, 559.
3. Verbrugge, *NIV Theological Dictionary*, 559.

This validates that to achieve *makarios*, one must be *teleios* which only stems from a covenantal relationship with God.

The idea behind *teleios* within the Hebrew equivalents in the Old Testament does not present the idea of moral perfection but rather an intimate stance with God. In the Greek Septuagint, the word *teleios* is used for multiple Hebrew equivalents, unlike *makarios*, which is used for one Hebrew word, *'asrê*. In the Septuagint, "all instances of *teleios* mean unblemished, undivided, complete and whole."[4] Within the Septuagint, *teleios* occurs over one hundred fifty times with such meanings as "forever" and "uttermost," all pointing to a state of fullness rather than perfection as modern society thinks of perfection.[5] The overlapping of the Hebrew words does not prove too broad of the meaning of what *teleios* is attempting to reveal. Pennington describes this group of Hebrew words that *teleios* reveals as the "tel-word" group.[6] Each presentation of the word *teleios* presents one central idea of wholeness or completeness that is not derived from human effort but a mature and intimate relationship with God. *Teleios* connects the Bible's recurrent theme of salvation as human flourishing.[7] Pennington gives three concepts of human flourishing that are presented with the Hebrew words *'asrê* ("happiness"), *tamim* ("wholeness"), and *shalom* ("peace").[8] To be in a state of *'asrê*, *tamim*, and *shalom* describes someone who is *teleios* or in a covenantal relationship with God.

Shalom and *Teleios*

The English gloss for *shalom*, like *'asrê*, can be misleading. *Shalom*, generally translated into English as "peace," presents the idea of release from war, quietness, or the absence of hostility. Although the ideas presented in what society considers peace are benefits

---

4. Verbrugge, *NIV Theological Dictionary*, 75.
5. Verbrugge, *NIV Theological Dictionary*, 559.
6. Pennington, *Human Flourishing*, 70.
7. Pennington, *Human Flourishing*, 70.
8. Pennington, *Human Flourishing*, 71.

Section One: A Correct View of *Makarios* Leads to a Correct View

of *shalom*, *shalom* presents a picture of someone who has inner peace due to *teleios* or their convental relationship with Yahweh. Much like *'asrê*, which stems from a covenantal relationship with God after he draws that person to himself, *shalom* stems from this relationship which is described by the Greek word *teleios*.

Tamim and *Teleios*

Pennington addresses another word, *tamim*, that when combined with *shalom* and *'asrê* brings *teleios*. *Tamim*'s use in the Old Testament presents the idea of integrity and singleness that results in wholeness or maturity. Like *shalom*, wholeness is again presented here but achieved through "integrity and singleness."[9] The word is seen when describing Job in Job 1:1 as a "blameless" man. The Greek word used to translate *tamim* in the Greek Septuagint is *amemptos* which means to be "blameless, or without reproach."[10] Job's intimate relationship with God was revealed through his blamelessness and reputation of being above reproach. The root of the word *tamim* is used to describe the condition of a person's inner being which is blameless and has integrity.[11] The one who is thus blameless, fortunate, and having inner peace is the one who is in a state of *teleios*.

Tying *'Asrê*, *Bārûk*, and *Teleios* Together

Tying *teleios* together with *makarios* reveals God's favor bestowed upon the believer. *'Asrê* and *bārûk*, though differing, also tie together through the word *teleios*. To be in a state of completeness, wellbeing, and singleness of mind, God's blessings must be bestowed upon them not due to their morality but by grace alone, which results in a state of *makarios*. God's blessing or *bārûk* is his revealed word; this is why the psalmist would say in Ps 1:2

9. Pennington, *Human Flourishing*, 72.
10. Liddell et al., *Greek-English Lexicon*, 81.
11. Brown et al., *Hebrew and English Lexicon*, 1071.

(although using the word '*asrê* in the beginning), "But his delight is in the law of the Lord; and in his law doth he meditate day and night." It is the blessing or *bārûk* of God's revealed word that transforms man's heart that results in '*asrê*.

8

Conclusion

GOING BACK TO THE rich young ruler presented at the beginning of section one, Christ's call is seen as a call not to moral perfection but *teleios*. Although this man had riches and strived to follow God's law, he was still searching for eternal life. Although the rich young ruler had riches and strived to fulfill God's law, he was not *makarios* but had the mindset that *teleios* was gaining wealth and completing perfectly God's law. Christ offered him *makarios* by giving him directions to obtain *teleios* or a covenantal relationship with him. The rich young ruler would have to sacrifice his thoughts of human flourishing, which was that of accumulating riches. He would also need to eliminate his legalistic mindset of working to receive God's blessing or *bārûk* and instead follow Christ. Following Christ leads to *makarios* or a state of human flourishing, yet the rich young ruler assumed he was already in a state of flourishing due to his many riches. Unfortunately, he would not let go of his temporary state of flourishing to gain eternal flourishing in Christ. He was not alone in thinking that God had blessed him with much due to his attempt in following the law of God; the Pharisees also thought that God's favor and blessing was bestowed based on human merit.

Conclusion

The Pharisees and those who sought human flourishing and God's blessings by legalism did so based on double-mindedness on how they should live that would both benefit them and offer honor to God. Their double-mindedness is seen by their desire to have God's blessings while having a life of riches and status. Self-sacrifice, which is what Jesus called his followers into, would require these Pharisees to rid their idea of achieving God's blessings and *makarios* through their traditions and legalism. Their fear of self-denial and self-sacrifice drove them to potentially view Christ's Beatitudes as a reversal of what they have always considered desirable to receive God's blessings. Understanding the words *makarios* and *teleios*, however, reveals that God's blessing is not achieved by merit; rather, God's blessing of a state of human flourishing results from *teleios* or having an intimate relationship with him.

Understanding that *makarios* cannot be achieved by merit frees believers of their role in salvation and dissolves the yoke of legalism. The view of having to constantly work to obtain God's favor leads to a life that is not flourishing but a life that is burdensome due to its commitment to legalism. Viewing the Beatitudes as a list of objects to achieve to receive God's blessings leads to a man-centered approach to salvation. With the wrong view of the Beatitudes, works-based salvation is unavoidable, and even if one determines himself saved, he thus has to keep working to keep God's blessing.

Christ states in Matt 11:28–30, "Come unto me, all *ye* that labour and are heavy laden, and I will give you rest. Take my yoke upon you, and learn of me; for I am meek and lowly in heart: and ye shall find rest unto your souls. For my yoke *is* easy, and my burden is light." The burden or yoke presented within this verse by Christ contrasts with the heavy yolk of Legalism.[1] The Pharisees at the time followed not only the 613 Mitzvot laws but also extra man-made laws, that if followed correctly would lead to God's blessings upon them.[2] They believed they had to achieve moral perfection to keep their favor with God. These laws acted as fences around

---

1. Walvoord, *Matthew*, 209–10
2. Rand, "613 Mitzvot."

Section One: A Correct View of *Makarios* Leads to a Correct View

God's law that were implemented to protect God's law from being broken. The idea of perfection bled over from the Pharisees to the society who shared moral perfection's burden. During the time of Christ, human flourishing was dominated by legalism, the idea that man has to help God in keeping their salvation. True freedom is found in what Christ says in Matt 11:29–30: "Take my yoke upon you. . . . For my yoke is easy, and my burden is light." Christ shows us in this statement that in the absence of legalism, *teleios* is obtained, leading to *makarios*. The yoke of Christ is *teleios* or a covenantal relationship with him that is "easy and light," providing a flourishing state due to dependence upon Christ. Understanding the Greek word *makarios* leads to the realization that *makarios* is not obtained through merit but is pure grace in God calling one into a covenantal relationship with him, thus releasing the burden of the false view of achieving perfection, allowing for freedom in Christ.

Understanding that *makarios* describes a state of being rather than a bestowed blessing is crucial to how a preacher preaches the Beatitudes. The preaching of the Beatitudes should not confuse the word *makarios* to mean a bestowed blessing by God but rather a state of being that is ultimately due to God's revelation to humankind. There is danger of preaching legalism if the Beatitudes are interpreted in such a way that denotes a list of duties a person must fulfill to receive God's blessing, much like the alternate views presented above by Scot McKnight and Danny Akin. This is easily done by trusting in the English gloss "blessed" rather than understanding that *makarios* is correctly interpreted to reveal a state of being. Correctly preaching the Beatitudes is to preach them as states of being that are due to God's blessing in revealing himself to us. This allows the preacher's congregation to see that true happiness and completeness stem in their covenantal relationship with Christ rather than how much morality they can achieve. Since God has revealed himself to man, those who obtain salvation are genuinely flourishing or are in a state of *makarios* because of their future inheritance to come and their status in Christ. Section two will describe the dangers of preaching the Beatitudes as qualities

Conclusion

to be met or strived for to receive God's blessings while showing the benefits of preaching the Beatitudes as qualities of those who are happy in their most total sense. Section two will introduce three dominant views of the Beatitudes and how they are used in preaching, while also providing an alternate view which fully captures what the Beatitudes represent. Section two will examine three dominant interpretations of the Beatitudes as mentioned by Jonathan Pennington in his book *The Sermon on the Mount and Human Flourishing*:

1. God's Bestowed Blessings/Entrance Requirements
2. Eschatological Reversal Blessings
3. Wisdom or Virtue Ethics Reading

A fourth interpretation will also be considered that blends multiple interpretations of the Beatitudes for preaching them properly as indicative statements rather than imperatives. Each view will have an example of how preachers have preached the Beatitudes and examine how it could have potentially affected their congregations.

Section Two

Four Dominant Views in Preaching the Beatitudes

9

Introduction

PREACHING THE BEATITUDES AS a description of those who are in a state of flourishing due to their relationship with God rests on the proper interpretation of the Greek word *makarios*. Jonathan Pennington rightly refutes that *makarios* means a bestowed blessing by stating that "*makarios* or *makarisms* are pronouncements, based on observation, that a certain way of being in the world produces human flourishing and true happiness."[1] Trevin Wax, professor at Wheaton College, states concerning *makarios*, "The opposite of a *macarism* is not a 'curse' (which would be the opposite of 'blessing'), but a 'woe,' and not surprisingly, in the final major discourse of Jesus we find in Matthew's gospel, woes are pronounced in Matthew 23."[2] Wax demonstrates the correct interpretation of *makarios* by giving its antonym which is a woe instead of a curse. Since a woe demonstrates a life of agony, *makarios* must demonstrate a life of flourishing. Section one examined the proper interpretation of the Greek word *makarios* by looking at its use within the Old Testament Greek Septuagint. *Makarios* within the Old Testament was used to translate the Hebrew word *'asrê* rather

1. Pennington, *Human Flourishing*, 42.
2. Wax, "True Human Flourishing," para. 10.

Section Two: Four Dominant Views in Preaching the Beatitudes

than the Hebrew word *bārûk*, proving that *makarios* is used to describe a state of being rather than a bestowed blessing. Section one also examined the proper interpretation of the Greek word *makarios* by looking at its use within the Old Testament Greek Septuagint. Section one continued to examine the fallacy of glossing *makarios* over with the English word "blessed." The rendering of *makarios* as "blessed" rather than the words "happy" or "flourishing" allows one to interpret the Beatitudes as qualifications that need to be met to receive God's bestowed blessings. Viewing the Beatitudes as qualifications leading to God's bestowed blessing encourages preaching the Beatitudes as a list of duties to perform rather than reasons why the saved individual is flourishing.

A correct hermeneutic when exegeting the Beatitudes allows for the Beatitudes to be preached as an encouragement rather than a burdensome list of qualifications that must be met to receive God's favor. The correct hermeneutic of the Beatitudes rests in one's interpretation of the Greek word *makarios*. How a preacher preaches the Beatitudes determines how he will preach other wisdom literature presented throughout Scripture, like the proverbs and even the Epistle of James. Indeed, the perspective of the entire canon of Scripture can be influenced by how one reads and interprets the Beatitudes. One's doctrine of soteriology rests in how one interprets the Beatitudes, viewing salvation as either a result of merit or a state given by God through grace alone.

Danny Akin provides eight interpretations of the Beatitudes which are also mentioned in section one, providing many examples of different interpretations one can take when exegeting the Beatitudes. The eight interpretations are (1) Utopian Ideal Ethics, (2) Millennial Ethics, (3) Spiritual Elite Ethic, (4) Eschatological Ethic, (5) Call to Repentance Ethic, (6) Principles of Life for Kingdom Citizens, (7) Intentional/Eternal Ethic, and (8) a Perfect Standard for the Christian Life.[3] Akin's last interpretation contrasts with a common misinterpretation of the Beatitudes that Pennington and McKnight present in their commentaries on the Sermon on the Mount. The common misinterpretation is a mixture of

---

3. Akin, *Exalting Jesus*, 15.

Introduction

some aspects of the previous seven interpretations that Akin presents his readers with, known by McKnight and Pennington as the "God's Favor View." McKnight claims that those who interpret the Beatitudes through the lens of the "God's Favor View" interpret the Beatitudes as a list of standards that, if performed correctly, will result in God's blessings.[4] According to Pennington, this view can also be called "The Beatitudes as Entrance Requirements."[5]

Pennington narrows down the many interpretations Akin presents to three dominant views of the Beatitudes. Each of Pennington's and Akin's views has its foundation in how the Greek word *makarios* is interpreted, namely from the root of the Hebrew words *'asrê* or *bārûk*, as mentioned in the previous section. Pennington lists three dominant views of the Beatitudes: (1) God's Favor, (2) Eschatological Reversal Blessings, and (3) Wisdom or Virtue Ethics Reading. Which view a preacher takes concerning the beatitudes will determine whether he preaches them either in a legalistic or an encouraging manner. This section will examine the three dominant interpretations of the Beatitudes mentioned by Pennington. For each view and interpretation, examples of sermons will be given to show how each view affects one's preaching of the Beatitudes. Lastly, this section will reveal the proper way to preach the Beatitudes as a combination of views 2 and 3 within Pennington's list of interpretations.

---

4. McKnight, *Sermon on the Mount*, 32.
5. Pennington, *Human Flourishing*, 60.

10

God's Favor/Entrance Requirements

PREACHERS WHO DO NOT study the original languages can easily glean the idea that the Beatitudes are entrance requirements by overemphasizing the English gloss "blessed" at the beginning of each Beatitude. The word "blessed" gives the connotation that whatever following the command or direction given is to be performed to receive such blessing from God. As mentioned in section one, two Hebrew words are glossed over frequently with the English word "blessed": 'asrê and bārûḵ. 'Asrê presents a state of flourishing or happiness while bārûḵ presents a bestowed blessing from God. The preacher must distinguish between the two and how they relate to the Greek word makarios. The misinterpretation that the Beatitudes are directions to receive God's favor stems from viewing makarios as a gloss to the Hebrew word bārûḵ.

According to Pennington, "Not all scholars understand makarios as being about God's favor, but many do."[1] Failing to interpret makarios through its foundational use in translating the Hebrew word 'asrê rather than bārûḵ can lead to dangerous interpretations which leads to dangerous preaching. Those who preach the Beatitudes with an understanding of the word makarios as

1. Pennington, *Human Flourishing*, 60.

God's Favor/Entrance Requirements

God's favor have the danger of preaching that God's favor and even salvation is earned by performing the Beatitudes listed. Preaching human effort to obtain God's favor is often associated with legalistic preaching, which often in the case when preaching the Beatitudes as entrance requirements.

Some commentators view the Beatitudes as God's favor but deny that they are entrance requirements. Charles Quarles, professor of New Testament at Southeastern Baptist Theological Seminary, states in his commentary on the Sermon on the Mount that the Beatitudes "define the character and conduct of those whom God has already claimed to be his children. They describe the holy life that necessarily results from genuine salvation."[2] Quarles does not state that the Beatitudes are entrance requirements but rather that salvation results in these characteristics or traits. Pennington points out another commentator, David Turner, who, like Quarles, claims that the Beatitudes are traits of those who have received genuine salvation.[3] Others, however, continue to hold the God's Favor interpretation of the Beatitudes and claim that the Beatitudes present a list of entrance requirements.

John Kobina Louis, a priest of the Archdiocese of Accra, reveals his interpretation of the Beatitudes after providing a sermon on eight of the beatitudes, saying, "In short, then, with the eight Beatitudes, St. Matthew depicts what he sees as the program of life that Jesus expects believers to follow in order to enter the kingdom of heaven."[4] He uses many illustrations to solidify his claim within his sermon. One illustration that Louis uses indicates that he interprets the Beatitudes using the God's Favor view. Louis says regarding his illustration,

> For the entry requirements to any of the universities in Ghana, a Senior High School student is expected to have a minimum passing grade of C6 (credit pass) for three core subjects and three elective subjects, out of eight subjects taken in the West African Senior Secondary

---

2. Quarles, *Restoring Christ's Message*, 40–42.
3. Pennington, *Human Flourishing*, 60.
4. Louis, "Beatitudes," para. 1.

Section Two: Four Dominant Views in Preaching the Beatitudes

Certificate Examinations (WASSCE). Unlike the grouping of WASSCE subjects, there are no "electives" among the virtues of the Beatitudes. In other words, they are all "core subjects" for all believers. One cannot pick and choose the virtues they like and leave out the rest.[5]

An example of legalistic preaching that directs men that salvation or blessing is obtainable through merit is presented within Louis's sermon. Such preaching can easily go to the extreme in declaring that one's salvation and hopes for eternal life rest not on the work of Christ alone but on one's merit. The weight of salvation thus is shifted from the Christ and his cross to Christ mixed with the merit of the one receiving salvation. Such preaching places a heavy burden upon congregants that salvation and God's favor rests heavily on one's actions rather than mainly in grace. Pennington rightfully points out this danger when he states that the "God's Favor/Entrance Requirements" view of the Beatitudes can be understood legalistically with a "mechanistic, tit-for-tat view of God: if you do X then God will favor you and give you Y."[6]

Robert Guelich states that there are two options for interpreting Matthew's Beatitudes: either they are "entrance requirements" for the kingdom or they are "eschatological blessings" inherited in the coming of the kingdom.[7] Guelich claims, "On the practical level, one frequently hears comments about trying to live according to the Sermon on the Mount. This generally means orienting one's attitudes and conduct by the various Beatitudes. The Beatitudes have become an ideal for human conduct, a goal to be pursued."[8] This type of preaching, Guelich states, leaves a congregation "with a sense of guilt or inadequacy."[9] Stanley Hauerwas, former professor of ethics and theology at Duke Divinity School, opposes the type of preaching this view produces. Hauerwas claims, "The temptation is to read the Beatitudes as a list of virtues that good people

5. Louis, "Beatitudes," para. 2.
6. Pennington, *Human Flourishing*, 60.
7. Guelich, *Foundation for Understanding*, 71–84.
8. Guelich, *Foundation for Understanding*, 71–84.
9. Guelich, *Foundation for Understanding*, 71–84.

ought to have or as deeds they ought to do. We thus think we ought to try to be meek, poor, hungry, merciful, peacemakers, or persecuted. Yet we know it is hard to try to be meek: One either is or is not. It is even more difficult to have all the characteristics of the Beatitudes at once! Yet, that is not what it means to be blessed."[10] Hauerwas is correct that attempting to accomplish each Beatitude every day as a requirement to receive God's favor leads to a life of great difficulty and ultimately fails to provide a state of *makarios*, but rather creates a state of resentment towards God. Such an interpretation of the Beatitudes and other similar Scriptures concerning promises to God that leads to a burdensome lifestyle are mainly taken by those in denominations with either a works-based salvation system intact or a belief that one's salvation is to be maintained by God plus their efforts or merit. This view also leads to the belief that to have this blessing, one must continue being as the Beatitudes present daily, or one's blessing will be removed. Such a view that places great weight on man's responsibility teaches that man is not totally depraved and can muster the strength to meet the moral standards presented in the Beatitudes to receive God's blessing. Thus, anyone who acts according to the Beatitudes and continues to do so will receive the kingdom of heaven.

Some in extreme branches of Arminian theology believe in partial depravity which implies that humankind has just enough of morality within them to choose God freely. This is crucial in understanding why many denominations who hold to extreme forms of Arminian theology misinterpret the Beatitudes. Some of these denominations believe humankind can choose to live a holy life based partially on their strength and partially on God's preserving power. This belief system, if applied to the Beatitudes, leads to trusting that conformity to the Beatitudes and keeping them till one dies will lead to a complete salvation. Contrarily, not conforming to the Beatitudes will lead to the loss of your salvation and a reversal of God's blessings. To preach the Beatitudes as entrance requirements that are supposed to be met to gain heaven diminishes the joy and assurance of salvation. The joy of

---

10. Hauerwas, *Reign of God*, 157.

Section Two: Four Dominant Views in Preaching the Beatitudes

salvation is thus robbed by anxiety of conforming as closely to the Beatitudes as possible to hopefully enter the kingdom of God. The human flourishing or happiness described within the Beatitudes is also lost if taken as measures one must meet each day to keep their ticket to heaven.

11

Eschatological Reversal Blessings

ANOTHER VIEW THAT PENNINGTON claims is common amongst modern scholars is called Eschatological Reversal Blessings. This view argues that the Beatitudes represent a reversal of fortune that Jesus promises to bring about in his future kingdom.[1] With this view, there is a proper understanding of how the Greek word *makarios* relates to the Hebrew word *'asrê*, meaning that *makarios*, like *'asrê*, reveals a state of flourishing or happiness. However, when reading the Beatitudes, scholars consider this view to understand that a complete state of human flourishing or happiness only occurs in the future when Christ ushers in the kingdom of God.

The foundation of this view is rooted in Isa 61, where the prophet speaks of how beneficial it will be for those living in God's kingdom. Isaiah opens chapter 61 saying, "The Spirit of the Lord GOD is upon me; because the LORD hath anointed me to preach good tidings unto the meek; he hath sent me to bind up the brokenhearted, to proclaim liberty to the captives, and the opening of the prison to them that are bound." It almost appears as if Isaiah is talking about those whom Christ is talking about in the Beatitudes, namely: those who are poor in spirit and those who are meek. The

---

1. Pennington, *Human Flourishing*, 60.

Section Two: Four Dominant Views in Preaching the Beatitudes

remainder of Isa 61 speaks of how these downtrodden folks will eventually be restored to a better condition, a state of true flourishing in God's coming kingdom that Christ will usher in. Pennington rightly states that "the language about the *Makarios*-ness of 'mourning' and 'hungering and thirsting for righteousness,' along with the promises of 'inheriting the land' and 'being satisfied,' are examples of the thoroughly eschatological vision of Isaiah."[2] The Eschatological Reversal Blessings view provides future hope for true flourishing that cannot be fully obtained now.

This view is taken up in denominations such as the Episcopal Church. The Episcopal Church's dictionary claims, "The Beatitudes are usually interpreted as a paradox, comparing the difference between present and future. Those who suffer or are poor now are blessed (or happy) because they are destined to be saved in the future when the kingdom arrives. The mercifulness and goodness of God will be demonstrated in the future."[3] In his sermon "An Exposition of Matthew 5:1–12," English Puritan preacher Thomas Watson called the Beatitudes "blessedness in reversal."[4] Watson would say in his illustration, "Alas, the tree of blessedness does not grow in an earthly paradise,"[5] revealing his stance that the blessedness provided in the Beatitudes is not current and does not stem from the current world but a future kingdom to come. Watson says regarding a coming blessing resulting in our deportation from the world, "Let us so deport ourselves, that we may express to others that we do believe a blessedness to come, and that is by seeking an interest in God. For the beams of blessedness shine only from his face. It is our union with God, the chief good, that makes us blessed. Oh, let us never rest till we can say, 'This God is our God forever and ever'" (Ps 48:14).[6] Watson also says in his sermon, "Yet many are digging for felicity here, as if they would fetch a blessing out of a curse; a man may as well think to extract oil out of a flint,

---

2. Pennington, *Human Flourishing*, 61.
3. Episcopal Church, "Beatitudes," para. 1.
4. Watson, *Beatitudes*, 11.
5. Watson, *Beatitudes*, 12.
6. Watson, *Beatitudes*, 16.

Eschatological Reversal Blessings

or fire out of water, as blessedness out of these terrestrial things."[7] Watson is correct in stating that blessedness and happiness do not stem from earthly materialism but from God alone; however, this leaves the listener with no direction for their current state of living while in the world.

Robert Guelich takes a similar approach to Watson when claiming that the Beatitudes are prophetic rather than concerned about wisdom ideals today.[8] The preaching of the Beatitudes as Eschatological Reversal Blessings is half correct in that it provides hope for the believer's future but leaves the believer with no direction on why they can live a flourishing life now. The listeners of Watson and Guelich would have hope in their future but no hope for the present. This view leaves the preacher scrambling to give exhortation on how one must bear suffering and heartache in this world while remaining hopeless for the present but hopeful for the future. David Garland, professor of Christian Scriptures at Baylor University, claims the condition presented within the Beatitudes "has nothing to do with the pursuit of happiness or with fortunate external circumstances but has to do with openness to the gracious activity of God to save his people."[9] Like Watson and Guelich, Garland, who holds the Eschatological Reversal Blessings view, leaves no hope for the present. Pennington agrees that there is an "Isaianic kingdom-restoring eschatological backdrop to the Beatitudes, but this in no way undercuts the vision of human flourishing that the Beatitudes speak to."[10] The error in this view is that it leaves no direction for the present while only giving hope for the future.

---

7. Watson, *Beatitudes*, 12.
8. Guelich, *Foundation for Understanding*, 71–84.
9. Garland, *Blessings and Woes*, 79.
10. Pennington, *Human Flourishing*, 63.

12

Wisdom or Virtue Ethics Reading

WHERE ESCHATOLOGICAL REVERSAL BLESSINGS speaks of a future hope of human flourishing upon the consummation of the second coming of Christ, the view of the Wisdom or Virtue Ethics Reading speaks to present human flourishing. As stated earlier, the context of the Beatitudes falls in the mixture of Greco-Roman virtue ethics and Second Temple Judaism wisdom literature.[1] With this context intact, the Beatitudes can be viewed as wisdom literature much like James, Proverbs, and Hellenistic literature from writers such as Plato and Homer. Humankind has always sought human flourishing, which is thought to be achievable through the step-by-step directions offered within wisdom literature such as Proverbs. Pennington states regarding the goal of human flourishing by those of Greco-Roman and Second Temple Judaism backgrounds, "The DNA of this tradition encodes the understanding that true flourishing can be found only in the context of 'the fear of the Lord,' and covenantal relationship with the one and only creator God."[2] Fearing God seems to be the foundational agreement and common trait in those who eventually obtain a state of flourishing.

1. Pennington, *Human Flourishing*, 66.
2. Pennington, *Human Flourishing*, 37.

Wisdom or Virtue Ethics Reading

Unlike Second Temple Judaism, Greco-Roman philosophy emphasizes ethics and how ethics leads to true human flourishing. Ethics in the Greco-Roman philosophy describes how to live a certain way in the world that births true happiness; thus, there is a high ethical stance that the Sermon on the Mount places on the person, leading to seeking salvation through human effort. In an interview, Jonathan Pennington states that "Jesus was not giving demands on how one should live to be able to enter into the kingdom of God but rather was speaking against the Pharisees whose hearts were far from God and who were not truly living a life of flourishing that comes from Christ."[3] Pennington also states, "Christ gave directions not to obtain salvation, but how to live a life that honors him and offers true happiness for the believer."[4] Pennington also claims that the Beatitudes have their foundation in the thrust of the Bible's teaching of morality and ethics. Pennington claims in his thesis called "The Moral View of the Bible Is a Revelatory Virtue Ethic,"

> The Bible shares with many of its contemporary philosophies and religions the understanding that ethics or morality is agentic and aretegenic. That is, ethics is about who people are and a certain way of being in the world, about becoming more virtuous as the means to flourishing. The Bible's goal in this virtue ethics is particular; however, in being eschatological and universally missional, it is not just about the individuals' human flourishing but also about God's restoration of *shalom* to the world.[5]

Pennington's view of the Beatitudes as a mixture of Eschatological Reversal Blessings and Wisdom or Virtue Ethics reading is the proper way to preach and view the Beatitudes, which will be discussed in the latter portion of this section.

Church history shows that preachers and theologians like Augustine and Thomas Aquinas hold the view that the Beatitudes

---

3. Brown, Jonathan Pennington personal interview, March 10, 2022.
4. Brown, Jonathan Pennington personal interview, March 10, 2022.
5. Pennington, *Human Flourishing*, 298.

are a part of the wisdom tradition, particularly in the Aristotelian virtue tradition.[6] Augustine's focus within the Scripture and particularly the Beatitudes was morality, and his understanding of morality is focused on the pursuit of happiness, which can only be found in God.[7] Like Augustine, theologian Servais Pinckaers in his devotional exposition of the Beatitudes continues to explore the great human question of how to obtain true happiness. In his exposition, Pinckaers explains that the Beatitudes offer best practices to live for Christians in the current world to have true happiness.[8] In chapter three of his book, *The Pursuit of Happiness God's Way: Living the Beatitudes*, Pinckaers connects the Beatitudes with holistic spiritualism that leads to a moral life. Pinckaers claims that the "Beatitudes challenge one's perception of true happiness and that true happiness is only obtained in the people of God."[9] Pinckaers also states, "We need no one to teach us that good fortune and joy will make us happy, but what we could never have discovered for ourselves is that poverty and suffering could be the most direct road to happiness and that Christ has chosen them as our way to the kingdom."[10] In Pinckaers's view, true happiness comes from a detachment of worldly standards like what is presented within the first Beatitude, that those who are poor in spirit will be blessed.[11] The thrust of such preaching is how one can obtain true happiness presently while being a Christian in a fallen world.

One advantage of preaching the Beatitudes this way is that it further validates that the word makarios is properly glossed over with the English word "happy" or "flourishing" rather than blessed. In the Greco-Roman context of virtue ethics, to achieve human flourishing, it is correctly considered that *makarios* does mean a state of human flourishing rather than a bestowed blessing from God. Unfortunately only Preaching the Beatitudes as

6. Pennington, *Human Flourishing*, 61.
7. Pennington, *Human Flourishing*, 300.
8. Pinckaers and Noble, *Pursuit of Happiness*, 35.
9. Pinckaers and Noble, *Pursuit of Happiness*, 35.
10. Pinckaers and Noble, *Pursuit of Happiness*, 35.
11. Pinckaers and Noble, *Pursuit of Happiness*, 35.

Wisdom or Virtue Ethics Reading

directions on living happily as a Christian in a fallen world while providing hope for the present leaves out the hope of a restored kingdom that provides true human flourishing, as the Eschatological Reversal Blessings view presented earlier. Humans will always seek to answer the question of how to be truly happy in the current moment, and the Beatitudes provide the answer to their question.

13

Blending Views of Beatitudes for Proper Preaching

EACH VIEW PRESENTED EARLIER regarding the Beatitudes has advantages and disadvantages within preaching. The view of God's bestowed blessing or the Beatitudes as entrance requirements can lead to legalism. Being incorrectly glossed over with the English word "blessed" has led many to believe that the Beatitudes are to be strived for and completed to enter the kingdom of heaven. To properly preach the Beatitudes however, God's bestowed blessings cannot be left out. The blessing that God has given is God's revealing of himself through his word which changes the heart of the man or woman who, in result, lives a life as presented within the Beatitudes, producing true happiness.

Pennington rightly addresses the error in ruling out God's bestowed blessing when preaching the Beatitudes. Pennington claims, "Thus, while it is important to realize that *'asrê/makarios* casts a vision of human flourishing, it is equally important to see that this flourishing can never fully occur apart from a proper relationship with the creator God."[1] The blessing is not that God

1. Pennington, *Human Flourishing*, 50.

Blending Views of Beatitudes for Proper Preaching

will grant someone eternal life due to their adherence to the Beatitudes, but rather God has implanted a new heart in the beatific person and given them a renewed mind to live as a new creation in Christ. For example, the person whom God has changed will recognize they are "poor in spirit" and in need of God, according to the first Beatitude. Thus, when believers acknowledge that God is the only one that can fill their bankrupt hearts, they become happy, because their happiness no longer rests in the temporal things of the world, but the eternal God who saved them. These who are "poor in spirit" will also find joy in God's promise that the kingdom of God is theirs currently and not just a future hope. Interestingly, the first Beatitude is written as a present indicative statement, meaning that Christ is indicating that presently these who are "poor in spirit" currently have the kingdom of God. So, while there is a difference between *'asrê/makarios* as human flourishing and *bārûk* as a bestowed blessing, they are connected, in that authentic human flourishing cannot be obtained apart from God's blessing.

While Pennington calls for not ruling out the view of God's bestowed blessing, he under-develops the reasoning behind this bestowed blessing. This blessing is not bestowed due to the believer becoming whatever the Beatitudes describe; but rather, due to repentance, the believer is blessed by God in his or her transformation into the person the Beatitudes describe. The Sermon on the Mount is a sermon addressed to believers who have repented and placed their faith in Christ; thus, God has blessed them by transforming them into citizens of the kingdom of Heaven.

Pennington correctly sees the Sermon on the Mount in its entirety as an exposition of Jesus's call for repentance. However, his insight is not adequately developed in his exposition, leaving the reader to question what the basis is for holding on to the God's Bestowed Blessing view. Jesus's urgent demand for repentance in view of the arriving kingdom of heaven must be described and revealed to the hearer, providing them grounds for not ruling out God's bestowed blessing while keeping an eschatological focus blended with wisdom literature when preaching the Beatitudes. Stephen

Section Two: Four Dominant Views in Preaching the Beatitudes

Bauer, professor of theology and ethics at Southern Adventist University, agrees that Pennington lacks reasoning as to why God bestows a blessing on those presented within the Beatitudes. Bauer addresses the lack of emphasis on repentance as the main driver in holding on to the God's Bestowed Blessing view of the Beatitudes. Bauer states in his review of Pennington's book *The Sermon on the Mount and Human Flourishing*, "At the very least, the first four of the Beatitudes appear to be an unpacking of repentance with its longing for righteousness, while the next four/five describe the fruits of repentance."[2] Repentance is a crucial component that the Beatitudes present that provides reasoning for also holding to the God's Bestowed Blessing view. Repentance is result of true faith in Christ, thus salvation cannot be obtained without genuine repentance. Therefore, if salvation is not intact, then the promises of the Beatitudes have no bearing on the unsaved individual. God's blessings and a state of flouring are interconnected not so much in a merit-based system but as one cannot happen without the other.

Psalm 1 and Ps 119 relate the Hebrew word ʾasrê ("state of flourishing") to those who study or meditate on God's word. The connection between God's word and ʾasrê is a given within Ps 1 and Ps 119 and proves that apart from God's *blessing* in revealing of himself through his word, one cannot obtain a true covenantal relationship with him that produces human flourishing. Pennington confirms that both Hebrew words ʾasrê and bārûk are connected within Scripture when he claims, "A God-oriented person is in a state of flourishing precisely because he or she is experiencing the most direct means of grace that God has ordained to effect favor upon His people, a meditation on God's self-revelation, or in short, knowing God."[3] Psalm 1 and Ps 119 are also considered wisdom literature, however they do not give direction on how to obtain blessing but rather show that due to God's blessing in revealing himself to his people through his word that they are in turn in a state of flourishing. Psalm 1 and Ps 119 are examples of passages

2. Bauer, "Human Flourishing," 132.
3. Pennington, *Human Flourishing*, 50.

Blending Views of Beatitudes for Proper Preaching

that blend the aforementioned views: God's Favor, Eschatological Reversal Blessings, and Wisdom or Virtue Ethics Reading.

The Beatitudes should be preached with God's blessing of revealing himself in mind. Preaching should emphasize that the effect of God's word changing people's lives through salvation results in the saved individual living in accordance with what the Beatitudes represent. It is not a matter of *if* a person lives according to the way presented in each Beatitude to receive God's favor, but rather that when God blesses them with salvation, they will naturally live in a way that reflects the Beatitudes, leading to human flourishing.

A preacher should maintain the God's Bestowed Blessing view, meaning that God has blessed in revealing himself while keeping an eschatological focus blended with wisdom literature when preaching the Beatitudes. Focusing only on the eschatological implications of the Beatitudes leaves the congregation with only a future hope of obtaining true flourishing when God ushers in his kingdom during the second coming of Christ. However, while only on the wisdom literature aspect of the Beatitudes provides a framework for how to obtain flourishing in the present but leaves out the future hope of complete happiness when God's kingdom arrives. Both views need to be blended and preserved when preaching through the Beatitudes. The question of what to do within the present to reach a state of flourishing will be left unanswered by focusing only on the Beatitudes' eschatological implications. Thus, the preacher needs to blend both views properly to help his congregation understand that the Beatitudes are not only future promises that one can hope in but promises that affect the present as well for those who are in Christ. Both views offer a correct interpretation of *makarios* within the Beatitudes as a state of being rather than a bestowed blessing but differ on when that state of being comes about.

While Pennington rightly addresses how believers can flourish in the present by holding on to the God's Bestowed Blessing view of the Beatitudes, he does not continue explaining why believers can have hope in their future as well. Matt Jones, associate professor of New Testament at Colorado Christian University, agrees in his review of Pennington's book that Pennington does not provide a connection between each Beatitude and present and future flourishing. Jones states, "I left each chapter wanting more of a connection between the commentary and human flourishing."[4] Flourishing in the present depends on two factors: our hope that God has blessed us with salvation and our present/future hope of an inheritance that is promised within the Beatitudes. By addressing the tenses used within the Beatitudes, the preacher will find that there is a present hope and a future hope given to the believer regarding his or her inheritance that will provide flourishing both in the present and the future. For example, those who are persecuted for the sake of Christ, as presented in Matt 5:10, already possess the kingdom of heaven. Pennington fails to mention this present-tense focus within his commentary, which would solidify his claim that believers can flourish in the present. The *eimi* verb in verse 10 is in the present active indicative, indicating presently those who have been persecuted have the kingdom of heaven.

The future tense is also represented within the Beatitudes. The rewards for certain Beatitudes, namely those presented in verses 4–9 of Matthew chapter 5 are presented in the future tense, namely the future passive indicative, thus providing future rewards that believers will obtain. Bauer agrees in his review of Pennington's book that "with as much attention given to the Beatitudes, there is no attention given to the difference in verb tenses of the bookend Beatitudes, emphatically in the *present* tense (5:3, 10), from the verb tenses of the enclosed Beatitudes, uniformly *future* tense (5:4–9)."[5] Thus, interpreting the Beatitudes correctly by using both views is solidified when the preacher makes note of the verb tenses.

Robert Guelich narrows down the Beatitudes to just mere prophecy about the future state of man in the coming kingdom of God. Guelich states, "The Beatitudes are not about wisdom ideals concerned with well-being but rather are prophetic."[6] Another

---

4. Jones, "Book Reviews," 387–89.
5. Bauer, "Human Flourishing," 133.
6. Guelich, *Foundation for Understanding*, 71–84.

theologian, David Garland, properly glosses *makarios* with the English word "happy," yet still maintains an eschatological view only of the Beatitudes. Garland's article "Blessings and Woes" translates the Beatitudes overall as "happy are the unhappy for God will make them happy."[7] Garland adequately addresses the condition of humankind as what the Beatitudes are presenting, but when that condition comes about is where Garland narrows his focus on the future. Garland continues in his article to say, "This condition that the recipients of the Beatitudes find themselves in has nothing to do with the pursuit of happiness or with fortunate external circumstances. It has to do with the openness to the gracious activity of God to save his people."[8] Garland is giving a future reference of God saving his people in the coming of his kingdom, thus making them become happy. He denies, however, that the Beatitudes focus on the present condition of man pursuing happiness. Garland and Guelich are correct that there is an Isaianic, kingdom-restoring eschatological backdrop to the Beatitudes, but this cannot dissolve the current human condition and the direction to obtain human flourishing in the present that the Beatitudes also represent.

The Second Temple Jewish context considers both views because Second Temple Jews relied heavily on wisdom literature to understand how to obtain happiness while still focusing on Jewish prophecy in hopes of God's coming restored kingdom. According to Pennington, Grant Macaskill's discussion on Jewish wisdom literature has shown that "in the Second Temple period, the strands of the wisdom tradition and of the apocalyptic and eschatological traditions are inextricably interwoven."[9] This means that in reading and preaching the Beatitudes, there needs to be an overlap between the view of the Beatitudes as wisdom literature for now and prophecy concerning the future.

In the latter chapters of Matthew, Jesus blends both wisdom and prophecy in his exhortation to his disciples when speaking of

7. Garland, *Blessings and Woes*, 79.
8. Garland, *Blessings and Woes*, 79.
9. Pennington, *Human Flourishing*, 63.

Section Two: Four Dominant Views in Preaching the Beatitudes

the coming end of the age. In his prophecy of the Second Temple's destruction in Matt 24, Jesus begins to give directions or wisdom on how to navigate the coming end of the age. In Matt 24:3–5, he gives warning to his disciples regarding the coming of the kingdom: "And as he sat upon the mount of Olives, the disciples came unto him privately, saying, Tell us, when shall these things be? and what shall be the sign of thy coming, and of the end of the world? And Jesus answered and said unto them, Take heed that no man deceive you. For many shall come in my name, saying, I am Christ; and shall deceive many." Jesus is speaking prophetically in this chapter regarding the future end of the gentile age and the coming of the kingdom of God while at the same time blending in wisdom literature by providing direction to navigate through such a time. The Beatitudes are no different in their purpose: the entirety of the Sermon on the Mount offers wisdom literature by providing direction on how to live as citizens of the kingdom of God while at the same time, in the latter part of the sermon, providing a future focus on when God will reject many because their hearts were far from him. Thus, the Beatitudes, like the remainder of the Sermon on the Mount and the Olivet Discourse presented in Matt 24–25, provide a blend of wisdom literature and eschatology regarding the end of the age.

Since the scope of the Bible, the Sermon on the Mount, the Olivet Discourse, and many other teachings from Jesus blend wisdom literature and eschatology, preaching the Beatitudes should blend both. Holding to both interpretations of the Beatitudes as wisdom literature and Eschatological Reversal Blessings allows for hope to be given for both the present and future condition of humankind. Preaching with both views intact presents the Beatitudes as promises that provide its hearers with both a present and future hope, allowing them to live a flourishing life in the present. Pennington rightly states, "Jesus is offering a vision for a way of being in the world that will result in true flourishing, precisely in the context of forward-looking faith in God eventually setting the world to rights."[10]

10. Pennington, *Human Flourishing*, 63.

Blending Views of Beatitudes for Proper Preaching

Ben Witherington is another commentator who agrees with a blended view of interpreting the Beatitudes. Witherington observes, "Jesus is a prophetic sage who uses the Old Testament in sapiential ways and at the same time reveals wisdom from God."[11] In his commentary on Matthew, Witherington states that the Sermon on the Mount is "a virtual compendium of the usual standing topics that sages would discuss," just like topics discussed within Proverbs and other wisdom literature.[12] Many commentators like Witherington confirm that the Beatitudes must not be viewed in light of one focus either as wisdom literature or prophecy, but both. R. T. France agrees that both views should be blended when interpreting and preaching the Beatitudes. According to Pennington, France also acknowledges the correct view of *makarios* as a state of being.[13] France claims in his commentary on Matthew that the people within the Beatitudes are "blessed by God" through his revealing of himself but are also happy in an "already but not yet way," proving that they are happy now but not in complete happiness that will be seen in the kingdom of God.[14]

---

11. Witherington, *Matthew*, 114.
12. Witherington, *Matthew*, 114.
13. Pennington, *Human Flourishing*, 111.
14. France, *Gospel of Matthew*.

14

Conclusion

LIKE R. T. FRANCE, who considers all three interpretations of the Beatitudes within his commentary on Matthew, the preaching of the Beatitudes should do the same. The preaching of the Beatitudes should not confuse the word *makarios* to mean a bestowed blessing by God but rather a state of being that is ultimately due to a bestowed blessing by God namely that of salvation. . The state which the Beatitudes represent is that of *shalom* or true human flourishing due to having a covenantal relationship with God that stems from salvation. In a rebuttal to the Pharisaic way of life of striving to be holy by completing a checklist of man-made laws, Christ presents the Beatitudes, as a profile for those who are the opposite of who religious leaders of Christ's day thought would enter the kingdom of Heaven.

Within the Beatitudes, God is seen as the ultimate provider of true happiness or flourishing. For example, in the second Beatitude, "Blessed [or happy] are the meek for they shall inherit the earth," Christ is saying that these who are lowly, gentle, and not aggressive in seeking out the things of this world—are the ones God gives the world. Many during this time assumed the earth belonged to the Romans and the religious leaders; however, Christ

Conclusion

promised those who were gentle and not warrior-like would inherit the earth. This promise provided security for the present and future end of the age. Preaching the Beatitudes with a blended view of all three interpretations not only provides security for the believer but also reveals the vast grace of God.

The Beatitudes show that God is gracious enough to bless his elect with his word and to reveal himself to his elect, causing them to be born again into a covenantal relationship which results in human flourishing. Within the first Beatitude, it is the "poor in spirit" who through this covenantal relationship with God realize that nothing can satisfy them apart from God; therefore, if they lose all and still have God, they will remain happy. The Beatitudes provide a present security for the believer because according to the first Beatitude the kingdom of heaven is already theirs. The Beatitudes also provide future security for the believer because as Christ promises in Matthew 5:8, these "will see God." When the preacher preaches the Beatitudes, he must show that the Beatitudes provide a profile describing believers, while also providing both present and future promises for the believer that provide hope for them in their current lives.

Section Three

Preaching the Beatitudes
for the Glory of God

15

Introduction

CORRECTLY INTERPRETING THE BEATITUDES provides encouragement to believers, showing that they can live a life in a state of contentment while suffering in a world that is anti-God and anti-Christian. Furthermore, the *macarisms* discussed in section one provide the framework to achieve flourishing amid suffering. Christ within the Beatitudes describes a state of flourishing that Christians can live in amid a fallen world due to their hope in their current citizenship of the kingdom of heaven and the future completion of God's ushering in of his kingdom. Understanding that each of the nine Beatitudes begins with a *macarism* is vital in understanding the latter part of each beatific statement. As stated earlier, the Beatitudes are not to be looked at as bestowed blessings but as invitations from Christ to live in a state of flourishing while waiting on the coming kingdom of God. Pennington rightly states that "macarisms are proclamations that invite the hearers into a way of being in the world (a vision of virtues) that promise human flourishing."[1] Presented within the Sermon on the Mount, the Beatitudes can answer the age-old question of how to be truly happy while living within fallen conditions.

1. Pennington, *Flourishing*, 150.

16

Macarisms and Other Scriptures

IT IS CRUCIAL TO examine the use of *macarisms* within and outside of Scripture to glean a deeper understanding of how to interpret them. *Macarisms* are not unique to the Sermon on the Mount but are also present in Scripture such as Ps 1, where the psalmist states, "Blessed is the Man." Immediately, the psalmist gives a *macarism*, not saying that God will bestow a blessing if one completes what is in the remainder of the psalm but rather the actions that are presented in beginning section of this psalm is the result of salvation which brings about a flourishing life. Second Temple Jewish writings, as well as Near Eastern literature in general, also contain *macarisms*. Ulrich Luz, former theology professor at the University of Bern, states that beatitudes present within wisdom literature other than the Sermon on the Mount show a "connection between a person's deeds and what happens to the person."[1] The Jews were heavily persecuted during the Second Temple period, so they formed many apocalyptic writings to give a future hope to a battered Jewish society. Interestingly, in the remainder of Matthew's Gospel, particularly in 10:16–23, Christ begins to warn his disciples that they are going to suffer for his name. In

---

1. Luz et al., *Matthew 8–20*, 187.

these verses, Jesus claims that his disciples are going to be sent out among wolves and be dragged by their enemies before governors and kings, suffering for his sake. Maybe the news that Christ gives them was a little more bearable as they considered the previous current and future promises Christ gave them in the Beatitudes earlier in Matt 5. Therefore, the Beatitudes should be preached in such a way that offers folks hope and comfort amid their suffering or coming suffering. The reality of suffering should never be negated in preaching but revealed in such a way that shows believers can suffer well once they realize their place and promises within the kingdom of God, as the Beatitudes presents.

Scripture confirms in multiple places that those in Christ will suffer for Christ. For example, John gives an account where Christ promised suffering in John 15:20: "Remember the word that I said unto you, The servant is not greater than his lord. If they have persecuted me, they will also persecute you." Peter, however, in his first epistle, gives a great example of how flourishing can come amid suffering. In 1 Pet 4:14, he states that "if ye be reproached for the name of Christ, happy [*makarios*] are ye; for the spirit of glory and of God resteth upon you." In other words, you are in a state of flourishing because "the Spirit of glory and of God rests upon you," even though you have been slandered. The recipients of Peter's letter are also in a state of flourishing because Peter has reminded them of their salvation and how God has chosen them, even though the world had rejected them earlier in 1 Pet 1:1–6, where the promise of a future inheritance echoes some of the promises within the Beatitudes that provide hope amid suffering.

Scholars also consider James's letter as "a piece of wisdom literature, the New Testament equivalent of the Old Testament books of Proverbs and Ecclesiastes,"[2] providing insight on how to flourish amid suffering. For example, Jas 1:2–3 states, "Count it all joy when ye fall into divers temptations; Knowing this, that the trying of your faith worketh patience." James reminds his readers that a Christian can "count it all joy" or be in a state of happiness because he or she knows that this suffering has been appointed for

---

2. Ryken, *Literary Introductions*, 521.

Section Three: Preaching the Beatitudes for the Glory of God

their ultimate good, drawing them closer to God and glorifying God at the same time.

Further, in Jas 1:12, James presents a *macarism* involving endurance amid suffering, stating a phrase very similar to the beginning of Ps 1, saying, "Blessed is the man that endureth temptation: for when he is tried, he shall receive the crown of life, which the Lord hath promised to them that love him." The word translated "for" in this verse in the Greek Septuagint is the Greek word *hoti*, which, according to Pennington, is flexible and can translate to "because."[3] When *hoti* is translated as "because," the verse gives better reasoning as to why someone can be flourishing as they remain steadfast under trial. The verse can be translated as "Flourishing is the man that endureth temptation: because when he is tried, he shall receive the crown of life, which the Lord hath promised to them that love him." In the Sermon on the Mount, Christ recognizes that Christians are going to suffer living as kingdom citizens in a fallen world; thus, he gives them comfort early in the sermon by providing them a profile of who they are as Christians, namely as those who are recipients of these wonderful promises given in each beatific statement. Preaching the Beatitudes as the indicative statements they are will help explain to congregants why they should be living in a state of flourishing in a fallen world, namely because of the promises indicated at the end of each Beatitude.

---

3. Pennington, *Human Flourishing*, 155.

17

Do the Beatitudes Contradict Society's View of Flourishing?

READ ON THE SURFACE, the Beatitudes can seem a bit contradictory and against the grain of what many consider to be a happy life. Today, social media paints an artificial picture, showing a person living their best life now in the apparent absence of suffering. Suffering, however, is as much a part of life as happiness. For the Christian, suffering is a promise that cannot be avoided nor diminished. How a Christian handles suffering determines the type of life he or she lives for Christ while anticipating his return. Paul understood that suffering was a part of his walk with Christ but was able to flourish amid his suffering because of his future eschatological hope of God's coming kingdom. Paul says in Rom 8:18, "For I reckon that the sufferings of this present time are not worthy to be compared with the glory which shall be revealed in us." He goes on to encourage believers in Christ to wait patiently for this future glory knowing this future glory is going to far overshadow any suffering they have ever endured. Paul rightly understands that suffering is an everyday occurrence; thus he maintains that the suffering he is facing is one that is occurring at this "present time," not a future suffering nor one in the past, but one that is consistently afflicting him. This present suffering which Paul faces does not keep him downtrodden due to his consideration and hope in his future with Christ. Paul has a future focus in mind when writing this verse, understanding that his suffering is temporal and given by divine sovereignty, allowing his suffering not to define him. Paul had an eschatological hope in mind of a future kingdom to come when his body, with all its current aches and pains, will be restored and glorified. Paul understood that his salvation was secure in Christ even though he remained in this world in a decaying fleshly shell that resulted from humankind's fall. To Paul, the kingdom of heaven as the Beatitudes presents was already his, and each day that passed by, Paul was one day closer to this kingdom that was his.

Paul suffered great persecution during his ministry, describing it as such in 2 Cor 11:25, saying, "Thrice was I beaten with rods, once was I stoned, thrice I suffered shipwreck, a night and a day I have been in the deep." Paul is no stranger to suffering for the cause of Christ, yet he can flourish in the midst of this suffering because of his present hope in knowing that God has reserved for him a place in his future kingdom of heaven.

Another of Paul's letters that reveals the suffering he endured is his letter to the Philippians. When reading the last chapter of this letter, many often take Paul's words in Phil 4:13 out of context, where the apostle says, "I can do all things through Christ which strengtheneth me." Usually, Phil 4:13 becomes the basis of a motivational speech for football games, leaving one to hope that Christ is going to give them a winning touchdown. However, Paul uses this verse to show that he can do all things, including being content amid suffering, through Christ who strengthens him. To truly grasp Phil 4:13, one must read the previous verses that show Paul suffering yet with contentment. Regarding his suffering, Paul states the following, starting in Phil 4:12: "I know both how to be abased, and I know how to abound: every where and in all things I am instructed both to be full and to be hungry, both to abound and to suffer need. I can do all things through Christ which strengtheneth me." It is his hope in his current position in Christ and his future home in the kingdom of heaven that allows for Paul to live in a state *shalom*, a state of *makarios* amid low points and even high points in life where the temptation is to forget God and enjoy pleasure.

Paul's hope in Christ is what drives his state of flourishing, similar to the hope the Beatitudes offer by their promises at the end of each statement. Paul does not seem to be the poster child of someone who is living their best life now, nor does he seem to follow the worldly standards of flourishing by getting a good job, making a lot of money, and having a big family. Paul is flourishing however because of his hope in Christ and the kingdom which is to come.

18

Biblical Standards for Flourishing

THE BEATITUDES PRESENT IDEAS of flourishing that result from the opposite of what secular society teaches leads to "living your best life now." According to the Beatitudes, those flourishing are those who are "poor in spirit," "who mourn," "who are meek," and "who are starving for righteousness." To be "poor in spirit" does not seem to be a proper ingredient one must have to live their happiest life. Those "who morn" seem to demonstrate the opposite of what most would assume breeds true happiness. Pennington rightly observes what is taking place in seemingly contradictory statements within the Beatitudes, calling the supposed contradiction "Paradoxical Suffering-Flourishing."[1] Pennington continues to say, "When we drill down even further into Matthew's series of nine *macarisms*, we find a rich reservoir of black gold; the Beatitudes are situated in a Christ-centered, apocalyptic and eschatological understanding of the world; they present true human flourishing as entailing suffering as Jesus's disciples await God's coming kingdom that Jesus is inaugurating."[2] Christ not only spoke of a present persecution that the disciples were going to face but also one to come at the end

1. Pennington, *Human Flourishing*, 153.
2. Pennington, *Human Flourishing*, 153.

Biblical Standards for Flourishing

of the age. It is their hope in the indicative statements that Christ gives in the Beatitudes, such as inheriting the earth and presently being a part of the kingdom of God, that allows his disciples to suffer well when the time comes.

In a portion of the Olivet Discourse in Matt 24, Christ speaks of the persecution Christians will face at the end of the age before the consummation of God's kingdom. He begins the list of persecutions they will face in Matt 24:9, saying, "Then shall they deliver you up to be afflicted, and shall kill you: and ye shall be hated of all nations for my name's sake." For the elect in Christ, the question is not if they will endure suffering but how they will endure suffering. To endure suffering well, Christians must hold on to the promises presented in the Beatitudes that provide both a present and future hope: hope that rests in the preserving power of Christ and the promises that the kingdom of heaven, which is already theirs, will come, eventually eradicating all of the persecution and suffering they may endure.

As Paul states in his letter to the Philippians, "to die is gain," pointing towards the end of life as gaining all that has been promised by Christ to those who are in him. The end of life, to Christians, is the eschatological hope of the coming kingdom of God and inheriting a new body built for such a kingdom. Death is the last valley a Christian must tread before entering the kingdom of God, which is already theirs while they are living. This means that, like Paul, whatever condition the Christian finds themselves in, they can still flourish because their future hope is far greater than the suffering they currently endure: a future hope of inheriting the earth and living within a physical kingdom of heaven as the Beatitudes present. John Calvin rightly asserts that, unfortunately, many hold to the belief that true happiness stems from being "free from annoyance, attaining all their wishes, which leads to a joyful and easy life."[3] Pennington, like Calvin, points out the skewed foundation many hold for true happiness, believing that "true happiness is about their present emotional state."[4] Carl Trueman is

---

3. Calvin, *Matthew 5*.
4. Pennington, *Human Flourishing*, 153

right in his book *The Rise and Triumph of the Modern Self: Cultural Amnesia, Expressive Individualism and the Road to Sexual Revolution* when he states the world is living in a "therapy culture."[5] This simply means that a person's emotions, feelings, and sense of belonging are the center of their world, and their happiness takes the front row even at the expense of morality. Calvin, Pennington, and Trueman agree that the unbeliever's view of happiness is based on their emotional state and their current condition rather than in Christ and the present/future promises God gives to his redeemed. Suffering must come and be endured for believers to reach the future promises presented within the Beatitudes, and they are able to endure suffering due to present promises presented in the Beatitudes. In other words, believers can bear their present sufferings much easier knowing that they currently have the kingdom of heaven (Matt 5:3) and that after all of their suffering is finished, they will eventually "inherit the earth," according to Matt 5:5.

---

5. Trueman, *Rise and Triumph*, 19.

19

Beatitudes Positive or Negative

THE BEATITUDES DO NOT seem to give what many consider positive human flourishing conditions but are rather dark in their direction. Pennington seems to agree by saying, "Rather, what Jesus proclaims as being a state of flourishing includes many things that humanity naturally and even vehemently seeks to avoid: poverty of spirit, mourning, humility, hunger and thirst, mercifulness, and peacemaking, and especially suffering through persecution."[1] Pennington claims that the key to understanding this paradox in the Beatitudes is understanding the relationship between the "protasis and the apodosis."[2] The protasis of a sentence is the clause giving the condition in a conditional statement. In the case of "blessed are the poor in spirit, for theirs is the kingdom of heaven," the protasis is "blessed are the poor in spirit," while the apodosis, the consequent clause of a conditional sentence, would be "theirs is the kingdom of heaven." Pennington helps the reader to understand the relationship between the protasis and the apodosis by translating the flexible Greek word *hoti*, or "for" in most English translations, that links the two halves of each Beatitude with

1. Pennington, *Human Flourishing*, 153.
2. Pennington, *Human Flourishing*, 154.

"because."[3] Pennington claims "because" shows that the apodosis provides the essential explanation or casual grounds for the radical paradox being claimed in the protasis.[4] The word "for," which many translations use as a weak English gloss for *hoti*, does not explain how flourishing derives from such lowly states and thus makes no sense. However, when translators use "because" in place of *hoti* or "for," we can clearly see an effect due to the cause, bringing clarity to each of the nine *macarisms* in the Beatitudes. With Pennington's translation of *hoti* as "because," we can read the first Beatitude as "flourishing are the poor in spirit because theirs is the kingdom of heaven." No matter how poor they are in spirit, no matter how lowly they are, these folks are possessors and citizens of God's kingdom which should give them hope.

Beatitudes and Their Future and Present Hope

There is present and future hope intact when the Beatitudes are understood correctly by considering the connection of their protasis and apodosis. The poor in spirit can flourish now because they are currently a part of God's kingdom and are hoping for its future consummation, which will even further validate their position. This future hope proves that the Beatitudes rest on Isaiah's prophecy of a restored kingdom to come, where Isaiah sums up the future hope that is given to those who serve Christ.

In Isa 60:18, the prophet claims concerning the coming kingdom of God that "violence shall no more be heard in thy land, wasting nor destruction within thy borders; but thou shalt call thy walls Salvation, and thy gates Praise." This eschatological promise of a kingdom where there is no more violence or destruction within its borders gives hope to those amid constant suffering and pain. Isaiah prophesies the fall of Judah and Israel but then shows that God will restore and protect them from their enemies. Judah and Israel would be captured and destroyed many times,

---

3. Pennington, *Human Flourishing*, 155.
4. Pennington, *Human Flourishing*, 155.

given over to multiple enemy nations for turning their backs on the Lord, yet God would always deliver them and never cast them off. Isaiah 60 confirms God's eternal bond with Israel, showing that even well on into the future Israel will be a part of the kingdom of God. Isaiah in Isa 60:19 prophesies that the kingdom of God is coming, and when it comes, Israel will be a nation that will see no more violence and there will be no more need for sun nor moon because "the Lord shall be unto thee an everlasting light, and thy God thy glory." These statements validate the apodosis of the first Beatitude that even though they are "poor in spirit," "theirs will be the kingdom of heaven." The poor in spirit can live in true *shalom*, inner peace and assurance that leads to flourishing because they are currently citizens of God's kingdom and will continue to be so when the kingdom is fully consummated.

In the New Testament, Peter's first epistle further confirms the Christians' promise of an inheritance of a future kingdom, solidifying the hope of the "poor in spirit" presented in the Beatitudes. In 1 Pet 1:4, Peter reaffirms the promise of a future glory and salvation to believers by saying that God has elected them and saved them "to an inheritance incorruptible, and undefiled, and that fadeth not away, reserved in heaven for you." Notice this inheritance is for those who are "begotten" or born again "to a lively hope by the resurrection of Jesus Christ from the dead"(1 Peter 1:3); thus this promise of an inheritance is meant only for believers in Christ. Peter uses three adjectives connected by two *kai* prepositions contrasting how this heavenly inheritance far outperforms any earthly inheritance. While earthly inheritances eventually fade and depreciate over time, the promised inheritance for God's elect that Peter describes is "incorruptible, undefiled, and fadeth not away." The Greek word for "incorruptible" is *aphthartos*, meaning this inheritance cannot be corrupted and is not subject to decaying. The New Testament uses this same word only seven times and twice to describe God as "incorruptible" in Rom 1:23 and "immortal" in 1 Tim 1:17. The usage of this word proves that this inheritance or future kingdom of God does not depreciate over time nor decays, unlike the treasures on earth. Christ confirms the eternality of the Christians' future inheritance and their need to desire it instead of earthly treasures when he says in Matt 6:19, "Lay not up for yourselves treasures upon earth, where moth and rust doth corrupt, and where thieves break through and steal." Christ assures believers that materialistic things will eventually fade and are corrupt, solidifying his call for believers to live joyfully knowing that they currently have the kingdom of heaven as theirs (Matt 5:3), a kingdom that will never fade, nor will it ever be corrupted.

Beatitudes and Salvation

Understanding who God's elect are and those whom he has saved is key to understanding who the Beatitudes are directed towards. The first Beatitude read on the surface seems to denote a person who is poor in spirit as receiving blessing from the Lord. Automatically the mind of those who heard Christ's beatific beatitude statements wonders, "How can I become poor in spirit to receive blessing from the Lord?" So how does one become poor in spirit? If the view of the Beatitudes is that of a checklist for how one must perform to receive salvation, then one must strive with their own efforts to make themselves poor in spirit. This interpretation of Christ's message is misleading and can lead to a life of legalism striving to become what Christ has presented in his beatitudes. To understand what the phrase "poor in spirit" entails, it is important to understand the Greek word *makarios*. Christ, again, is talking about a state of being, namely *makarios*, denoting that truly happy are those who are poor in spirit, not those who attempt to be poor in spirit, which would be miserable to attempt. Taking the first Beatitude into consideration, *makarios* is the adjective, which means it follows the linking verb "are" and describes the subject of the sentence, which in Matt 5:3 is "the poor in spirit." The subject of this indicative statement in Matt 5:3 are the *ptōchoi*, or the poor and needy. The article "to" after *ptōchoi* acts as a preposition, particularly a dative preposition meaning "to" or "with respect to." So those who are flourishing are those who are poor with respect to the spirit. Their salvation began with understanding that they are spiritually poor without Christ. One does not simply make themselves poor in spirit—all already are. The key however to living a life of flourishing is the realization of one's poorness of spirit without Christ. The foundation of one's salvation and what draws them to salvation is God's revealing to them their spiritual bankruptcy without him. Thus, those who are poor in spirit are those who God has shown that they are bankrupt without Christ, indicating that Christ has already dealt with their hearts and given them salvation. Regeneration has taken place in the one who has become poor in spirit. Their hearts have been changed to recognizing their poorness in spirit, and inserted within those hearts is faith that understands and seeks richness in spirit, which is obtained in Christ. To shed light on how Christ claims those who have already obtained salvation will be poor in spirit, leading to true happiness or *shalom* in the present, we must take the Old Testament into consideration.

20

Beatitudes Considering the Old Testament

CHARLES QUARLES, VICE PRESIDENT for Integration of Faith and Learning, claims that if we are to correctly interpret the Beatitudes, we must see them "in the backdrop of the most important pronouncements of blessings in the law of Moses."[1] Christ, at the beginning of his Sermon on the Mount, is pronouncing blessings, or key factors in living a life in a blessed state. Matthew and the writer to the Hebrews present Christ as a better Moses, as superior to Moses. So, naturally, the Beatitudes are superior pronouncements of blessings than what Moses gave in the Old Testament; however, to interpret the Beatitudes correctly, we should take Moses's pronouncements into consideration. Quarles helps his readers understand why the backdrop of Moses's pronouncements to Israel is important for understanding Jesus's pronouncement to his disciples. In Deut 33:29, Moses's final blessing on Israel appears when he states, "Happy art thou, O Israel: who is like unto thee, O people saved by the Lord, the shield of thy help, and who is the sword of thy excellency! and thine enemies shall be found liars

---

1. Quarles, *Restoring Christ's Message*, 40.

unto thee; and thou shalt tread upon their high place." Regarding this passage, Quarles states, "Israel's blessing had both a historical focus and a future focus. The words 'saved by the Lord' referred to Israel's exodus from Egypt."[2] As in the Beatitudes where salvation results in happiness or flourishing, in Moses's pronouncement, Israel's salvation in their exodus from Egypt occurred before they could be truly happy or in a state of *shalom* within the land that God provided for them. Salvation is key when understanding the characteristics that the Beatitudes portray. Those who are slaves to sin cannot be poor in spirit or meek, nor will they hunger and thirst for righteousness. The lost can attempt to portray a life characterized by the Beatitudes, but it will only be superficial while their hearts truly are not in the state presented within the declarations.

Quarles is correct when referring to Moses's pronouncement in Deut 33:29 as a backdrop for the Beatitudes when he states, "Matthew did not introduce Jesus as the New Moses in the introduction to the sermon only to abandon the theme immediately of His view of the Law.... The Beatitudes are more than likely a continuation of the New Moses theme than a temporary detour from the theme."[3] Jesus introduces Old Testament verbiage throughout the Beatitudes to bring familiarity and understanding to those who received them. Christ uses this example from the Old Testament to jog their memory, looking at how Israel went from enslavement to eventual freedom to live in a happy state in the land God provided. The same concept exists for those who are spiritually in exodus from their sinful state; they will eventually dwell in the kingdom of heaven. They are already citizens of heaven spiritually; thus, they can truly live happily in the present. This state of happiness the Beatitudes portray are due to a future hope and present status with God. According to Quarles, "This background suggests that the Beatitudes are not mere expressions of ethical principles accompanied by rewards but are pronouncements of salvation that identify Jesus's disciples as the new Israel."[4] Christ, in this sense,

---

2. Quarles, *Restoring Christ's Message*, 39.
3. Quarles, *Restoring Christ's Message*, 40.
4. Quarles, *Restoring Christ's Message*, 40.

Section Three: Preaching the Beatitudes for the Glory of God

is the spiritual deliverer of his people, much like Moses was the physical deliverer of his people from Egypt.

With a Mosaic backdrop attached to the Beatitudes, one should interpret the rest of the Sermon on the Mount not as a list of laws or duties one must check off to make it to heaven but rather as characteristics of those whom Christ has already saved. Quarles confirms this when he states regarding the commandments within the rest of the Sermon on the Mount, "They describe the holy life that necessarily results from genuine salvation. Jesus pronounced salvation on the disciples through the Beatitudes, then proclaimed the benefits of salvation in the ethical teaching that follows."[5] The Beatitudes and the remainder of the Sermon on the Mount are not something anyone achieves, but rather, these ethical qualities are the result of salvation, which is not achieved by man but by God. Foundationally, there are two views of the Beatitudes that reveal one's theology of salvation. The first view is that the Beatitudes are a checklist of things to complete to receive salvation. This view leads to a man-centered theology where man is in control of his salvation. The other view is that the Beatitudes are the result of God's overall blessing of revealing himself to man, thus saving the one who will inherit the kingdom of heaven. In this view, it is the change that God does to man's heart that results in the person the Beatitudes and the rest of the Sermon on the Mount describe. This view leads to a God-centered theology where God is in control over mankind's salvation because man is unable to save himself. It results from a proper understanding of mankind's total depravity, which makes any attempt to be the person the Beatitudes portray impossible for the one who is not genuinely regenerated.

Many Scriptures prove that humankind cannot accomplish what the Beatitudes portray or, more importantly, salvation. For instance, a popular Scripture proving man cannot save himself or live out the Beatitudes is in Paul's statements in Rom 3:10–12, stating, "As it is written, There is none righteous, no, not one: There is none that understandeth, there is none that seeketh after God. They are all gone out of the way, they are together become unprofitable;

---

5. Quarles, *Restoring Christ's Message*, 40.

there is none that doeth good, no, not one." Paul is not being rogue in his statements here, but Paul is quoting from the Old Testament. In this case, Paul is quoting directly from Pss 14:1–3 and 53:1–3, using Scripture to validate his claim of the extreme nature of the depravity of man. These statements alone that Paul and the psalmist make prove that man, in their own capacity, cannot perform what the Beatitudes portray. To be poor in spirit, to be meek, to be pure in heart, and to hunger and thirst for righteousness results from a heart already changed by God through salvation. If someone does not seek or understand God, then they cannot possibly hunger and thirst for righteousness without God first intervening. Only those whom God has caused to be born again will hunger and thirst for righteousness as presented in Matt 5:6. Proverbs 2:9 confirms that only God can bring a man to desire righteousness when Solomon states that it is only God who implants wisdom in the heart of man: "Then shalt thou understand righteousness, and judgment, and equity; yea, every good path." Thus, it is only through the saving knowledge of God that one can hunger and thirst for the righteousness that the Beatitudes present.

Another dangerous interpretation of the Beatitudes is that they not only must be achieved but they must be kept to receive the promise presented within each. Again, this view is heavily man-centered and stems from an extreme Arminian theological perspective that humankind not only has the libertarian free will to choose God but also has the option to choose to maintain their salvation through their righteous living. Again, this leads to a man-centered theology where man is responsible for keeping his salvation and thus not only performing the Beatitudes but striving every day to complete them so they can retain the kingdom of heaven as presented within the first Beatitude. As a result, the Beatitudes, along with salvation, become imperatives that provide conditions to those who keep these imperatives. Again, the Scriptures constantly refute the idea that man must keep his salvation while also, as in the case of Paul's statement earlier, refuting the notion that man can accomplish a certain lifestyle or display specific characteristics allowing him to receive salvation. Many Scriptures refute the belief that man must maintain salvation by checking off certain characteristics or laws the Bible gives. Instead, Prov 2 speaks of the godly wisdom that God gives to those whom he chooses. He gives this wisdom for the purpose of keeping them—or preserving them, in some translations—from evil. Proverbs 2:11 states that the result of God's granting such wisdom is that "discretion shall preserve thee, understanding shall keep thee." The word "preserve" stems from the Hebrew word *shamar*, meaning "to mark," "to preserve," "to reserve," or "to save." The Hebrew word presents many actions God performs through the wisdom he gives, preserving man and keeping them from evil, thus proving that man cannot keep or maintain his salvation. Moreover, numerous other Scriptures prove the doctrine of the preservation of the saints, further demonstrating why the Beatitudes should not be viewed as an ideal list of attitudes one must accomplish and maintain to receive salvation and keep their salvation.

21

Conclusion

THE BEATITUDES PRESENT A dilemma to those who have not obtained salvation, thus not experiencing the peace that the promises each Beatitude brings at their ending. How can one be happy yet be poor in spirit? The answer lies in God's granting salvation to an individual based on his will alone. This is where the Beatitudes present the grace God gives to the individual. The person can live a life of flourishing in a fallen world due to God's grace in giving them salvation. Many Scriptures also validate that it's God's will, not man's will, that results in one's salvation, proving that the Beatitudes—and the characteristics and benefits they portray—result from God alone and cannot be purchased with merit.[1] Once the Holy Spirit regenerates a person, they become poor in spirit, they become meek, they become lowly, they become pure in heart, and they begin to hunger and thirst for righteousness because God has redeemed them and given them a new heart. These folks are happy because of the rewards the Beatitudes present. As we stated above, it's easier to understand the Beatitudes if they are translated correctly as "happy or flourishing are the poor in spirit because theirs

---

1. Scriptures validating God's will in the salvation of an individual are John 1:13; 1 Cor 1:30; Eph 1:4; Phil 1:6; 2 Tim 1:8–9; Jas 1:18; 1 Pet 1:3, 23.

Section Three: Preaching the Beatitudes for the Glory of God

in the kingdom of Heaven." Reading and preaching them as indicative statements of promise rather than imperative statements will provide hope to the believer rather than a burdensome life of trying to achieve each Beatitude to obtain the promises that are given at the ending of each one. The Beatitudes are given to the saved as reminders that life in a world that is marred by sin does not have to be so bad, and the Christian can rejoice in their current state and their future state in Christ. The Beatitudes provide a profile for believers: who they are, what God has done for them, and what promises he has in store for them in the future. May all believers find rest and comfort in their salvation as they grasp hold of the Beatitudes.

Bibliography

Akin, Danny. *Exalting Jesus in the Sermon on the Mount*. Nashville: B&H, 2019.
Alexander, Thomas D., et al. *Dictionary of the Old Testament*. Downers Grove, IL: InterVarsity, 2003.
Aristotle. *The Nicomachean Ethics*. Translated by H. Rackham. Cambridge, MA: Harvard University Press, 2003.
Barry, John D., et al. *Faithlife Study Bible*. Bellingham, WA: Lexham, 2012.
Bauer, Stephan. "The Sermon on the Mount and Human Flourishing." *Andrews University Seminary Studies* 58 (Spring 2020) 130–34. https://digitalcommons.andrews.edu/cgi/viewcontent.cgi?article=3959&context=auss.
Betz, Hans Dieter. In *The Sermon on the Mount: Commentary on the Sermon on the Mount*. Minneapolis: Fortress, 1995.
Black, David A. *It's Still Greek to Me*. Grand Rapids: Baker Academic, 1998.
Botterweck, G. Johannes, and Helmer Ringgren. *Theological Dictionary of the Old Testament*. Grand Rapids: Eerdmans, 1980.
Brannan, Rick, trans. *The Apostolic Fathers in English*. Bellingham, WA: Lexham, 2012.
Brown, Francis, et al. *The Brown-Driver-Briggs Hebrew and English Lexicon*. Peabody, MA: Hendrickson, 2015.
Brown, Michael L. "רָשָׁע." In *New International Dictionary of Old Testament Theology and Exegesis*. Vol. 1. Edited by Willem A. VanGemeren. Grand Rapids: Zondervan, 1997. https://dokumen.pub/new-international-dictionary-of-old-testament-theology-and-exegesis-1-0310481708.html.
Bryan, Steve. "A Discourse on Human Flourishing: Henry Center." Henry Center for Theological Understanding, 2018. https://henrycenter.tiu.edu/2018/08/a-discourse-on-human-flourishing/.
Campbell, Constantine. *Advances in the Study of Greek: New Insights for Reading the New Testament*. Grand Rapids: Zondervan, 2015.
Carson, D. A. *Matthew*. The Expositor's Bible Commentary. Edited by Tremper Longman et al. Rev. ed. Grand Rapids: Zondervan, 2010.

Bibliography

Charry, Ellen T. *God and the Art of Happiness*. Grand Rapids: Eerdmans, 2010.
Clements, R. E. "Der Segen im Alten Testament. Eine Semasiologische Untersuchung der Wurzel Brk, by Gerhard Wehmeier. Friedrich Reinhardt Kommissionsverlag (Dissertation Basel VI), Basel, 1970. Pp. 244." *Scottish Journal of Theology* 25.2 (1972) 238–39.
Davies, W. D., and Dale C Allison. *Matthew 1–7: Volume 1*. International Critical Commentary. Edinburgh: T.&T. Clark, 2004.
The Episcopal Church. "Beatitudes." https://www.episcopalchurch.org/glossary/beatitudes/.
Ferda, Tucker, Daniel Frayer-Griggs, and Nathan C. Johnson, eds. *To Recover What Has Been Lost: Essays on Eschatology, Intertextuality, and Reception History in Honor of Dale C. Allison Jr.* Leiden: Brill, 2021.
Ferguson, Sinclair B. *The Sermon on the Mount: Kingdom Life in a Fallen World*. Carlisle, PA: Banner of Truth, 1997.
France, Richard T. *The Gospel of Matthew*. Grand Rapids: Eerdmans, 2010.
Freedman, David N., et al., eds. *The Anchor Bible Dictionary*. New Haven: Yale University Press, 2008.
Garland, David. "Blessing and Woe." In *Dictionary of Jesus and the Gospels*, edited by Joel B. Green et al., 77–81. Downers Grove, IL: InterVarsity, 1992.
Gemeren, Willem. *New International Dictionary of Old Testament Theology and Exegesis*. Milton Keynes, UK: Paternoster, 1997.
Guelich, Robert A. *The Sermon on the Mount: A Foundation for Understanding*. Waco, TX: Word, 1991.
Hartin, P. J. *A Spirituality of Perfection: Faith in Action in the Letter of James*. Collegeville, MN: Liturgical, 2017.
Hauerwas, Stanley. "Living the Proclaimed Reign of God: A Sermon on the Sermon on the Mount." *Interpretation* 48 (April 1993) 152–57. https://stanleyhauerwas.org/articles/living-the-proclaimed-reign-of-god-a-sermon-on-the-sermon-on-the-mount/.
Heer, Cornelis de. *Makar, Eudaimon, Olbios, Eutychēs: A Study of the Semantic Field Denoting Happiness in Ancient Greek to the End of the 5th Century B.C.* Amsterdam: A. M. Hakkert, 1969.
Hengel, Martin. *Judaism and Hellenism: Studies in Their Encounter in Palestine During the Early Hellenistic Period*. London: SCM, 1974.
Janzen, Waldemar. *'Ašrê In The Old Testament*. Cambridge, MA: Harvard Divinity School, 1965.
Jones, Matt. "Book Reviews." *Journal of the Evangelical Theological Society* 61.2 (2018) 387–89. https://www.etsjets.org/files/JETS-PDFs/61/61-62/JETS_61.2_367-433_Book_Reviews.pdf.
Louis, John. "The Beatitudes: Entry Requirements—Sunday Homily and Mass Readings." In *Homilies of Very Rev. Fr. John Louis*. https://www.bishoplouis.com/archives/2587/beatitudes-entry-requirements/.

Bibliography

Louw, Johannes, and Eugene Albert Nida. *Greek-English Lexicon of the New Testament: Based on Semantic Domains.* New York: United Bible Society, 1996.

Luz, Ulrich, et al. *Matthew 1–7: A Commentary.* Minneapolis: Fortress, 2007.

MacArthur, John. *Kingdom Living: Here and Now.* Chicago: Moody, 1980.

McKnight, Scot, and Tremper Longman. *Sermon on the Mount.* Grand Rapids: Zondervan, 2016.

McMahon, Darrin M. *The Pursuit of Happiness: A History from the Greeks to the Present.* London: Penguin, 2006.

Miller, Patrick D. "The Blessing of God." *Interpretation: A Journal of Bible and Theology* 29.3 (1975).

Mitchell, Christopher Wright. *The Meaning of BRK "to Bless" in the Old Testament.* Atlanta, GA: Scholars, 1987.

The NET Study Bible: Full Notes Edition. Richardson, TX: Biblical Studies, 2006.

Neusner, Jacob. *Christian Faith and the Bible of Judaism: The Judaic Encounter with Scripture.* Grand Rapids: Eerdmans, 1987.

Pinckaers, Servais, and Mary Thomas Noble. *The Pursuit of Happiness—God's Way: Living the Beatitudes.* Eugene, OR: Wipf & Stock, 2011.

Pennington, Jonathan. *The Sermon on the Mount and Human Flourishing: A Theological Commentary.* Grand Rapids: Baker Academic, 2017.

Plessis, Paul Johannes du. *Teleios: The Idea of Perfection in the New Testament.* Kampen: Kok, 1959.

Quarles, Charles L. *Sermon on the Mount: Restoring Christ's Message to the Modern Church.* Nashville: B&H Academic, 2011.

Rand, Archie. "The 613 Mitzvot." 2021. https://www.jmu.edu/dukehallgallery/exhibitions-past-2018-2019/the-613-mitzvot.shtml.

Rubin, Aaron D. "The Form and Meaning of Hebrew 'Asrê.'" *Vetus Testamentum* Vol. 60.3 (2010) 366–72.

Ryken, Leland. *Literary Introductions to the Books of the Bible.* Wheaton, IL: Crossway, 2015.

———. "Jonah." In *Literary Introductions to the Books of the Bible*, 313–20. Wheaton, IL: Crossway, 2015.

Spicq, Ceslas, and James D. Ernest. *Theological Lexicon of the New Testament.* Peabody, MA: Hendrickson, 1996.

Stott, John R. W. *The Message of the Sermon on the Mount.* Downers Grove, IL: IVP Academic, 1978.

Tesch, Noah. "Jesus and the Apostles Are Believed to Have Spoken Aramaic." In *Encyclopedia Britannica.* Chicago: Encyclopedia Britannica, 2002.

Turner, David L. *Matthew.* Grand Rapids: Baker Academic, 2014.

Tyndale, William. *Expositions and Notes on Sundry Portions of the Holy Scriptures: Together with the Practice of Prelates.* Edited by Henry Walter. Eugene, OR: Wipf & Stock, 2004.

Verbrugge, Verlyn D. *The NIV Theological Dictionary of New Testament Words: An Abridgment of New International Dictionary of New Testament Theology.* Milton Keynes, UK: Paternoster, 2000.

Bibliography

Vos, Geerhardus Johannes. *The Kingdom of God and the Church*. Grand Rapids: Reformation Heritage, 2001.

Wallace, Daniel. *Greek Grammar Beyond the Basics: An Exegetical Syntax of the New Testament*. Grand Rapids: Zondervan, 1996.

Walvoord, John F. *Matthew: Thy Kingdom Come*. Chicago: Moody, 1982.

Watson, Thomas. *The Beatitudes: An Exposition of a Puritan's Mind*. https://www.apuritansmind.com/wp-content/uploads/FREEEBOOKS/TheBeatitudes-ThomasWatson.pdf.

Wax, Trevin. "How the Beatitudes Invite You to Experience True Human Flourishing." The Gospel Coalition, June 12, 2017. https://www.thegospelcoalition.org/blogs/trevin-wax/how-the-beatitudes-invite-you-to-experience-true-human-flourishing/.

Wenham, Gordon J. *Rethinking Genesis 1–11: Gateway to the Bible*. Eugene, OR: Cascade, 2015.

Willard, Dallas. *The Divine Conspiracy: Rediscovering Our Hidden Life in God*. New York: Harper One, 2018.

Witherington, Ben, III. *Matthew*. Macon, GA: Smyth and Helwys, 2006.

Wright, N. T. *Interpreting Jesus: Essays on the Gospels*. Grand Rapids: Zondervan Academic, 2020.

www.ingramcontent.com/pod-product-compliance
Lightning Source LLC
Chambersburg PA
CBHW060030180426
43196CB00044B/2345